MW01612844

Grandmother Speaks

Deborah Laughing Heart Horbert

Grandmother Speaks

Copyright © 2011 by Deborah D. Horbert

ISBN 978-0-9742776-3-9

Rampart Press

Hendersonville, NC

A Personal Note:

This book is a record of my own experiences, conversations and lessons with Grandmother. It is not a book of instructions, or a how-to guide on becoming enlightened. Please take what resonates as truth now, leave the rest and perhaps consider coming back to it at a later date.

I have been advised by some people that perhaps I shouldn't be quite so open when relating my doubts and fears. The feeling was that it might make my experiences with Grandmother less effective. I disagree. For me, the fact that Spirit can use a person in spite of their human frailties is one of the things that make this book so engaging. If Grandmother can use me, then she can use anyone.

ACKNOWLEDGEMENTS:

With the deepest love and gratitude, I wish to acknowledge and honor my Medicine Woman, Chief Running Water of the Setalcott Tribe of Long Island, NY. Words cannot express how much her love and patience has healed me. Her teachings changed my life.

I wish to thank my husband Paul, for loving and supporting me through the writing of this book, and my adventures with Grandmother. I love you.

Thank you to my three incredible children, and my ten amazing grandchildren, all of whom inspire me more than they could ever know. I love you all so much. We are always connected by our heartstrings.

Thank you Robert for all of your help, your patience and for your editing skills. Thank you Cyndi for the hours you spent typing this manuscript and the lessons we learned together.

Thank you to the friends (you know who you are) who believed that this book needed to be written and encouraged me through the whole process. Thank you, Jane, for being so instrumental in helping me get Grandmother's message out to the public in the beginning.

Thank you Susan my spirit-sister, for the amazing artwork. I had a vision, and you brought it to life with your incredibly talented hands. Aho!

And finally to Grandmother, thank you for showing me how big I really am, and for honoring me with your messages.

LIGHT AND SPACE

SOUND AND BREATH

WEAVE THE WEB

OF LIFE AND DEATH.

FROM THE VOID

THE SPIRAL SPINS

NOW THE SACRED

DANCE BEGINS.

Foreword

I find Grandmother's stories and messages channeled by
Laughing Heart intriguing, meaningful and above all, in sync
with the energies of the changes currently taking place on the
Earth. It is a worldwide message to all humanity on all levels.
What a powerful teaching to realize that we are in the midst
of achieving higher consciousness as we adjust to a new
paradigm. The information channeled in this book is a
powerful tool for all of us as students of the Universe. I am
indebted to Laughing Heart for having the courage and honor
of accepting Grandmother into her being to spread the words
of Wisdom and Truth.

Anastasia Ethel Crites, B.S., M.ed.,

Guidance and Counseling, Medium, Spiritual Healer, and Writer.
Consultant to the Homicide Division, Washington, DC 1995-2000
Psychic Researcher with the Poseidia Institute, 1988-1990

PROLOGUE: SUMMER 1995

I had ventured away from the formalized Church several years ago, wanting more than it offered and my path had taken me to a Native American Medicine Woman named Joy and Happiness of Running Water. A series of extraordinary events resulted in me becoming her apprentice. I had been in training with her for several months when something wonderful and unexpected happened.

I spent literally thousands of hours with her over the next two years. Often after spending a day at her house, I would come home dizzy and nauseous, my mind spinning with the concepts that had been introduced to me. She systematically took my illusions of reality, one by one and completely shattered them. I needed some way to quiet my mind in order to absorb all that I was learning. To this end, I was attempting to incorporate the practice of meditation into my daily life, so there I sat with my legs crossed beneath me, feeling very uncomfortable physically. I was determined to put myself into some kind of trance which is what I perceived meditation to be at that point. It wasn't working. I was totally present, and completely aware of everything around me. However, as I just sat there, I opened my mind to being okay with just sitting there and that's when the wonderful and unexpected happened.

In my mind's eye, the picture of an old Native American woman began to form. The mental image was very clear and detailed. She had long gray braids, and was clothed in leather with intricate beadwork at the neckline of her dress. She wore a beautiful beaded necklace and prayer feathers in her hair. Her incredibly wrinkled brown face carried a gentle smile and was filled with ancient wisdom. Standing outside of her tipi next to the fire, she crooked her finger and gestured for me to approach her, which I did in amazement. She introduced herself as simply "Grandmother" and said she was my Spirit guide. Motioning for me to follow, she drew back the flap of the tipi, bent over and crossed the threshold. I entered behind her. The deliciously intoxicating smell of sage and sweet grass filled my nose as we sat facing each other in the semi-darkness. I inhaled it deeply as she began to speak, and so began our relationship.

She has been with me ever since, and if I listen, she will speak to me. This mental communication is how we conversed for nearly ten years, until I began to write down our conversations. These written pages were originally meant for me only. I wrote them down so that I could remember her words. I had almost convinced myself that I was just making her up and reading our conversations over at a later date helped me realize that I couldn't be making her up, because she spoke very differently than I do. I was writing down ideas and concepts that I knew weren't mine. I would read one of our conversations and think; *Wow, that was good! I didn't know that!*

Little by little, she encouraged me to read some of her messages to others. I hesitantly did as she asked, and they were always received with reverence. People realized that the words came from Spirit and that I was only a hollow bone for them to flow through.

More and more often I would sit down at the computer to talk with Grandmother. Without fail, she always had a message for me. I began to realize that these messages were applicable in a very universal way, not just for me personally. The friends that I shared her messages with said that they were encouraged and comforted by her words too.

Slowly the idea was born to put together the material in book form so that she could reach a larger audience.

You will find that Grandmother has a sharp wit and a quick sense of humor. My prayer is that you may discover as I did, hidden in the simplicity of her words, deep spiritual truths that offer comfort, wisdom and hope to a world in transition.

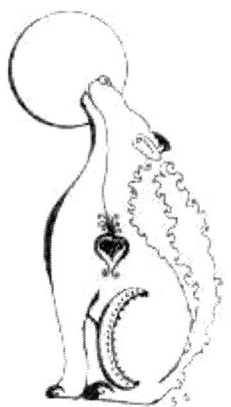

Spring 2006   Conversation One

Our first written conversation began while I was unemployed. I was feeling frustrated, unsure of myself and was at a loss about what to do. Not much in my life seemed to make sense right then, so I went to the one place where I felt safe and accepted. . . I went to Grandmother.

Hello, Grandmother. Well, here I am. What am I supposed to do now? Please talk to me.

I will always talk to you, child. You just do not always listen. If you are ready to listen now, then let us begin. You ask what are you supposed to do with your life. The answer is you are supposed to live it. Not wait until something comes along that you think is worthy to do, just do every day whatever is in your power to do. It does not have to be big, and you do not have to save the world. All you have to save is yourself.

What do you mean, save my self? How do I do that and what am I saving my self from?

You save your self by being yourself and you are being saved from not being who you really are. You

are a powerful, beautiful spirit and you do not even believe me when I say that. You have things to do and people to meet. A place in this world that no one but you can fill is waiting for you to fill it.

But how can I fill it if I don't even know what it is?

You fill it by beginning to be yourself, who you really are and how you know yourself to be. In your heart, you know yourself to be a wise and powerful healer, and yet you do not trust yourself to be that. In the days to come there will be much for you to do to help others realize who and what they are. But first you must come to those realizations about yourself. You look to other teachers for their wisdom. You want a medicine woman, or a visitation from the Goddess, complete with all the bells and whistles! You will not be quiet long enough to hear the sound of your own heartbeat and the wisdom in your own soul. You have lived many lives before and now is the time for you to make a big leap in your spiritual evolution. You have heard it from others and teachers have told you it is time to step into your eldership. You have even felt the physical symptoms of a great transformation that is taking place in your physical body. You know that you are vibrating at a much greater speed than you were before and that is why you are tired much of the time. It is not depression that you are feeling. It is Change. A change in your body, a change in your mind and a great change that is taking place inside of millions of people all over the planet.

Is this the change that is supposed to herald in the New Age after the Mayan calendar ends?

It is the very same. There will be many new things and new knowledge and a new way of being for all people who are willing to embrace it. New knowledge meaning that it is coming to light for the first time in thousands of years, not that ancient knowledge is being replaced. For indeed, there is no new knowledge, or new truth, for Truth simply IS. All knowledge exits in some dimension, whether it has come to light in your world or not. The Bible speaks of this time. Native American prophecy tells of this age and the Mayans foretold it. All New Age material has talked about it at some time or another. It is all speaking of the same time. A great Earth change will take place. There will be a cleansing of the Earth Mother as she goes into labor to bring forth a new body for her children to live upon. All of the natural calamities that you will hear and read of are supposed to happen, so that the Mother can be fresh and revived and ready to support life in a new way. People will live longer and be healthier, and will not be afraid of what they cannot see or understand. Knowledge will be readily accessible to all who seek it.

Your brothers and sisters from far away will be teaching you things they have already learned. Do not be concerned that they do not contact you now. When the time is right, you will know that they are here. All will know that they are here and have been here since the beginning. Indeed, they are the seed from which mankind has sprung.

Now see Grandmother, this is the kind of talk that scares me and makes me think that I am just making things up because I want so badly to hear from someone. Besides I was taught that God and not some aliens, created us all. How does God figure into this picture?

God is the central figure, my child. Did not God create all things? This is what you were taught, is it not? It is just that God as you were taught to view Him is not exactly how He really is. In fact, He is not really a He at all, or a She for that matter. Although the female noun is much closer to what God is than the masculine noun. God is primarily a creative force and that makes the energy more female than male. In reality, it is equal measures of both. This is the Energy that created all things, and sustains all things. It is God, it is the Life Force, it is the Universal Chi, it is the Great Mystery, the Source, the Creator, the I Am That I Am which holds all things together.

But I liked a God who was personal and cared about each individual and heard you when you prayed and answered you when you called!

Why do you think a God like I just described cannot do all of those things? Why do you think Creative Energy does not care about you? Why were you created at all if you don't count for something in the grand scheme of things? If you had some choice in the matter of when and where you incarnated on Earth and you did, then why did you pick now? Is it not because your soul knew that today is an exciting time to be on this planet? Did you not conspire with Creator to be here at this time and in this place? Most certainly you did! So stop fretting child and be assured that you have a purpose. There is a plan for your life. It is not a puzzle to confound you, nor a trick to confuse you. All that has transpired in your life up until this very moment in time is necessary for growth. Nothing has been without reason and purpose. Nothing has been mundane or ordinary, trivial or accidental. It was all pieces of your life plan

that were specifically designed and intended for your very best and highest spiritual growth. You took part in making this plan for your own soul. You cannot remember that now, but it is the truth. When you came to Earth to learn, you chose to forget who and what you really are. The years on Earth are a process of remembering those things.

Yeah, well if I knew so much, why did I want to come and be so miserable trying to remember something that I already knew in the first place? Why know something and then forget it on purpose and then come here to try and remember it? That doesn't make sense to me.

A lot of things don't make sense to you and yet they are true. Aerodynamics doesn't make sense to you, yet you will fly in an airplane when necessary. Electricity doesn't make sense to you, but you cannot do without it for one single night when a storm causes it to shut off! Do you understand my point?

I guess so, but that doesn't mean that I like it.

No one asked you to like it, or to understand it for that matter. Try and just accept it.

Okay, say that I accept the things you say as being true, at least for now. What happens next? What do I do about these things and when do I become this big healer person and how do I make a living in the meantime? I do have to make a living, don't I?

Make a living. What an interesting turn of phrase. How do I ask, does one make a living? Shouldn't one instead, live a living?

That's very funny, but you know what I mean. I have to have a job to earn money so that I can have a place to live and food to eat and a car to drive and that kind of thing. You have to admit it takes money to get along in the world today. And even spiritual events cost money. Some of these so-called spiritual events cost so dearly that only the very rich can avail themselves of the lectures or retreats or whatever. Why is that?

Maybe they need to make a living too.

Okay Grandmother, I can see that this is going nowhere, so let's change the subject.

I need and want specific answers to my questions, not some cosmic gobbledygook about universal love and aliens coming and energy and stuff like that. I need a job and I need something to do each day that makes me feel like I am doing something worthwhile. And no matter what you want to call it, I do need to make money or we can't keep our house or pay for the car or anything else. If I am being materialistic, then so be it. Because this is reality, in the world we live in now. Maybe the future will bring a change, but this is not the future, this is right now. And Grandmother, you know that I want to have a job doing something that is healing like Reiki, or having groups for women to help them find their power, or working with autistic people. I don't want some mindless, repetitive, boring job that burns me out and brings home a paycheck and that's all it does for me or anyone else.

I know that, child. I see your heart.

Grandmother, this is beginning to sound suspiciously like that series of books called *Conversations with God*. Am I just copying Mr. Walsch's' ideas?

What? I can't talk to more than one person at a time? If I am God, I can do anything I want to do, right?

Right. So does that mean I am talking to God?

You are talking to the one you refer to as Grandmother. I am your higher self, your inner wisdom, your spirit guide, God, Goddess. You pick.

Okay, I'm going to pick all of the above.

Good for you, because I am all of those things, and they are all the same. You are God, Goddess, your own wisdom, and your own spirit guide. God/Goddess is all that is and everyone is a part of that All-ness, a little piece of Me, if you will. It has been said that I break off a piece of Myself and send it to Earth to experience things since I can't really experience them because I AM all things, correct? But that is not exactly what happens when you are born. You choose to break away from Me, because you want to see for yourself what living as a single unit is like. In this way you can decide how to live your life. If you wish to stay divided, you can experience that here on Earth. If, however, you wish to return to that state of Oneness you can also do that. You can feel the Oneness there, in the third dimension, but never as fully as when you were here with Me, in a state of perfect completeness. At some point in time, all souls will return to that state.

But I still don't get it. If things were so perfect, why did I choose to leave in the first place? It just does not make sense to me! Oh wait, I remember, I don't understand a lot of things but that doesn't make them not true, right? And you never answered my question about getting a job that lets me use my gifts for healing and helping others. How do I go about doing that? I mean I can't just look in the paper for a job description that says, "We want someone to do Reiki and other healing things like that." can I?

Why not? Don't they have schools that teach Reiki, and places that offer Reiki treatments? Are you sure you're not just making excuses because you are afraid?

Afraid of what? You tell me, you're God! Yeah, okay and so am I! I know! Well, maybe I am afraid. Maybe I am afraid that if I really try to do something wonderful, I will fail. Suppose I get the perfect job that lets me use all of my gifts and I am not good at it after all?

Then what would I do?

Why would you not be good at it? If it is your gift, isn't it better to use it than to let it stagnate? Isn't that what really makes you fail? To have a gift and not use it to help people, which is what you keep saying you want to do? You will help some people and others you will not reach. That's why lots of people have gifts, and not just one or two people. If you had to help everybody in the whole world then maybe you should be scared, since that is a pretty big order for one person. All you have to do is help the ones who come to you, the people who cross your path every day. If you can't have a studio for Reiki right now, then give that loving, healing energy to the people you meet in Wal-Mart, at the post office and the gas station. It is good to dream and think big, but it is okay to start small, remembering that no healing is ever small. You touch one person with kindness and love and healing and they in turn pass it on to another person. The circle goes on and on and the ripples get bigger and bigger. Before you know it your small kindness or healing touch has spread out and touched twenty, thirty, or forty people. It is like the movie you liked so much, *Pay It Forward*. I inspired that movie, by the way. All

**inspiration comes from me. Look up the word
inspiration in the dictionary.**

I did. It says the act of *breathing in. The act or power of
arousing the mind or emotions.* So, all breathing in, all
inspiration comes from you. When I breathe I am inspiring, I
am taking in breath, right? I am arousing my mind and
emotions! I am breathing in the Divine! I can be inspired
every day just by breathing. Every breath is holy. Now I see
why the Native Americans knew that each and everything a
person did was holy and scared. They knew that every breath
was an inspiration of the Divine. It is an inbreathing of God.
A taking into themselves of the essence of the Great Mystery.
I see now why breath work has become so important and
popular in the last few years. It truly is the most important
thing we do and I don't mean for the obvious reason that we
can't live physically unless we breathe. I mean that conscious
breathing is what keeps us totally connected to God and
ourselves, or rather to the fact that with every breath we are
literally taking God into ourselves. We are returning to that
state of oneness from which we came. Each breath is a
miniature example of the cosmos!!

**Very good. That is correct. God is breathing the
universe into being and you are breathing God back
into yourself. It is a circle, as all things are. Creator
breathes out and creates and you breathe Creator
back into yourself. Look at Mother Earth for an
example. She is a living, breathing, organism, not
just a dead mass of rock and dirt. That is why it is so
important to be gentle with her and to treat her with
respect. She breathes and takes in breath, which is
God, or Life Force and so is inspired. Another way to
say inspired is to say be filled with the breath of God.
This is how she is able to sustain life and make
plants and trees and flowers grow out of her very
body. She breathes in the life of the Creator and then**

gives that life to the children of Earth. All your relations, four legged, winged ones, finned ones, two legged, creatures big and small, she breathes the breath of Creator into them.

That's pretty awesome Grandmother. It gives me a different perspective on the Earth and also on how we should treat her. Thank you.

Conversation Two

Now I have a question about something you said before, Grandmother. What exactly does stepping into my eldership mean?

It's about recognizing that you are a woman of wisdom. A woman who has lived for fifty seven years and has life experience that could be of benefit to others. You can share your experience with other women. Some experiences you can share with men because they are mutual experiences that everyone has, not just women. Others, you will share only with women. If you will step out and begin to teach by the way that you live, people will recognize you as an elder. You won't have to tell people who you are. They will know when they hear you speak and when they see how you live your life. You were being an elder when you helped your friend with her situation and took her children under your wing. Being an elder is primarily about tending to the younger ones. Physically, mentally, emotionally and spiritually tending to them. You have chosen to walk the Red Road and that makes you Native American no matter what percentage of Indian blood you carry in your veins. You have the actual physical bloodline, but that isn't what makes you Native American. It is a path you choose to follow. A path that embraces the sacredness of all creatures and all things. A path that knows the rocks, trees, plants and animals all have Sprit inside of them. They are living, breathing organisms that have a piece of the Creator in them. A path that respects all life forms and knows that all life is divine and holy. Do not take the life of any living thing if possible. If you can crush an ant beneath your feet without any feeling, it is only a matter of time until you can crush the life out of another form of being. How long before you are desensitized to killing in any form? How long does it take for someone to reach the place where they can kill another human being? Ancient people killed for food and clothing, not for sport. It is a spiritual exchange between two beings. One offers to sacrifice its self for the good of the community, or for the good of the other being. It is done out of mutual respect and out of caring for the welfare of another. The animal chooses to give its life for the support of the tribe. The hunter, then, takes that life respectfully and thankfully, knowing that it cost the animal ALL. He would never take more than he could use, or more than was needed. If any was left over, it was shared with other tribes. Nothing was ever wasted. In this way, there was enough for everyone and animals were not slaughtered needlessly. This is the old way.

So, the sacredness of life is an important teaching for the elders to give to the young.

Yes, one of them.

What is another one?

That life is eternal and never ending. There is no death. There is only a change of form. When the lessons of this world are learned, it is time to move onto another dimension and continue learning. Many ancient ones are in the spirit world and they teach us lessons that we need to know in order to move on. Some people refer to these ancient ones as spirit guides. You call yours Grandmother.

I thought Grandmother was God/Goddess?

She is, and all of the ancient ones are parts of God/Goddess too, remember?

Yes, I remember. Let me see now, the sacredness of life, and the fact that life is eternal are important teachings. What else?

That God/Goddess is all that there is. All things are God and God is all things. No one can worship another God because there is no other God. There is only One, and if you worship, then you are honoring the only true God. Remember when I told you many years ago that I know who I am and I will answer when I am called no matter what name my child calls Me by? Some people call you by your given name, your children call you Mommy your husband calls you Honey, and so forth. Yet you answer to all these names when you hear them, because you know who you are and you know that they are calling you. It is the same with Me. I hear someone call Me and I answer because I know who they are calling, no matter what name they use.

I love that illustration because I totally understand what you mean. You also talked to me about getting to a destination by different routes, or taking different roads to get to the same place. Can you tell me that again?

Of course. Now suppose that you live In New York, and your children all live in different parts of the country. You invite them home for Christmas, and they all come, but they get there by different means of transportation and use different maps. One flies in an airplane and gets there first. Another drives and it takes quite a while longer. The next one drives too but takes a newer highway, and arrives hours

before the other driver. When the children arrive, you are thrilled to see them and you make them welcome. Do you say to the one who drove, you came the wrong way, sorry but you can't come in? The important thing is that they got there!! That's all you would care about, right? Just be happy to see them and be glad that they arrived safely? Well, that's how I feel when my children make it safely home! And here is the best part . . . there's nowhere else they can end up, because all roads lead back to Me! You will all get here eventually, it is just a matter of when, and how difficult your journey is. The journey is the main event; it is the process of getting back that is important. The Sufi teachings that you love, speak of life as a wheel. Picture a wheel in your mind, with the hub at the center and the spokes radiating out in all directions. I am that hub at the center and all the spokes are connected to me. Start at the end of any spoke and follow it back to the center and there it is connected to the hub. All paths lead to the center, all paths lead to God. There is no other place to go. Do you see it?

I think I do, but it is scary, because it is not what I was taught growing up.

Have the things you were taught growing up made you happy, satisfied, or fulfilled? Did they not instead make you feel worthless, hopeless, and fearful?

Yes, they did make me feel that way.

Then perhaps, it is time to let go of the things you were taught growing up. Can you imagine how it would feel to be peaceful and calm and to know that you are loved all the time no matter what you think or feel inside about yourself? To know that you are valuable, worthwhile and have a purpose? Wouldn't that make you feel good? Well, all of those things are true. You know them in your mind, but your heart cannot accept the truth. Or rather to put it more appropriately, your heart and your soul know these truths. But your mind obscures them with logic and analytical thinking. You may read this information in a book, or hear it at some retreat and accept it as truth because you believe the person who told you, or the book you read. So your mind believes, but will not get out of the way so that the truth can get down into your soul and reawaken it to what it has always known.

I went to bed that night with Grandmother's words ringing in my ears. It was a lot to process and so very different from the teachings I had received as a child growing up in the Baptist church. Fear and guilt were the cornerstones of my religious upbringing and I had embraced them without question. Now I had many questions, so the next day I sat down to talk with her again.

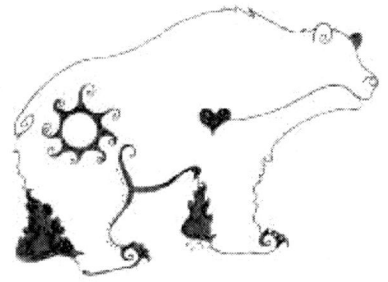

Conversation Three

Grandmother, could we talk some more about letting go of the things I was taught while growing up?

We can talk about whatever you wish to talk about, child. Let us start with your childhood beliefs. You were taught that if you did not love God you would go to Hell, correct? And you were told all the things that you could not do, all the things that would make God mad if you did them and then that's how you would wind up going to Hell.

Yes, that's mostly what I remember about going to church when I was a kid. I knew all the things I wasn't supposed to do, but I had no clear idea of what I *was* supposed to do. And I knew that most of the things I couldn't do were the fun things that I would have liked to do! I remember being afraid of God and the story about the Rapture terrified me! I expected every day to come home and find everyone gone but me. I was going to be left behind because I was bad. I remember feeling that I was bad all of the time. I would want to go down to the altar and get saved every time the preacher gave an altar call, because I wasn't sure that the last time had really worked!!

So you loved God out of fear, would that be correct to say? You loved him because they told you that if you didn't love him you would go to Hell. Then they told you that you had free will and could choose whether to love Him or not. They said He gave you free will because He didn't want to force you to love Him but to love Him because you wanted to, right?

**But if you *didn't* love Him you would go to Hell!!
Now that's not such a great choice after all, is it?**

No, it wasn't. And even today I can feel remnants of that old
fear. Sitting here typing these words I can hear the whispers
in my mind that say this is blasphemy and I am going to Hell.
Will I ever be free of those old voices in my head?

If you choose to be, you can be free of them.

I want to be free of them, but I don't know how to be. It's like
the things you tell me sound wonderful, and I want to believe
them but I just can't. I say that I believe them and I accept
them in my head, but I can't seem to act as though they are
really true. It seems to me that if I really believed them, then
I would be able to live differently. I wouldn't be so scared all
the time. Scared that I might be doing the wrong thing,
scared that what I am doing is not what God wants me to do.
And of course, never knowing what it is that He wants me to
do.

**Listen carefully child. I will tell you what God wants
you to do. God wants you to be happy. He wants you
to do whatever it is that makes you happy. He wants
you to live a joyful, creative, energetic, magical and
spiritual life. Whatever you do that doesn't harm
others is okay with God.**

But I feel like I need guidance. That I don't know what to do
unless someone tells me what to do. I think I should do
something only if it's worthwhile-or helps others, or is very
important in some way. I'm tired of working just to make a
pay check and because I think I am supposed to have a job. I
really want to something creative, energetic, magical and
spiritual, but I don't know how because I don't know what it
is that I need to be doing!

What do you want to do? Tell me your idea of the ideal job for yourself.

Okay. Well, it would be something that would help others heal from past hurts. It would be fun and exciting, and make me feel like I really made a difference in somebody's life. It definitely is working with people and not doing something solitary. Maybe spending a lot of time outdoors with nature. I want to know how to use herbs for natural healing and I would like to know more about working with the energy of crystals. It would also involve music and the healing effect that sound can have on people. Oh and colors, I want to learn how to use colors for healing. I'd also like to have my work centered in Native American ways of being because they feel very right for me. So do you have any openings for a job like that?

I see that you are trying to be funny, but the truth is that yes, I have a lot of openings for just that very work you described. You have to look in the want ads for them. In other words, find where the need is for that kind of healing work, and then go meet that need.

You make it sound very simple. But it's not that easy. There is a lot of that kind of stuff out there these days and some of it is very bizarre. I don't want people to think that I'm a kook. Besides, I said I want to learn about a lot of those things, not that I already know them. How can I tell, or teach others something that I don't know myself?

You are drawn to these things because you have an innate knowledge of them in your spirit. All you need to do is access that knowledge. Of course you can study them too and read which you have always done all of your life. It is time to take all of your book knowledge and put it to use. Start with what you

know the most about. I believe that would be your knowledge of Reiki. Start a class, give some treatments, make those business cards you keep talking about and put them up where people can see them.

Where will I hold a class? How can I give treatments without a table that I can't afford? Who's going to come to me when Reiki practitioners are a dime a dozen? What makes me so different or special?

You have a very long list of excuses for not doing what you claim you really want to do. Why do you think that is? I already know, but let's see if you do.

Fear?

Excellent! Of course, fear. Fear is the biggest obstacle for any of you to overcome. It keeps you stuck in one place, and unable to move forward. Do you know what it is that you fear?

Failure?

That's what one would think, isn't it? But no it's not failure. What you really fear is success. You are afraid that you might be as wonderful and as powerful and as effective as you could possibly imagine. You are afraid that you may actually live up to your full potential. And then what? Suppose you still weren't fulfilled? What excuse would you have then for not being happy? It is a convenient excuse . . . I would be happy if . . . or I will be happy when . . . I am trying to tell you that you can be happy now, plus have the joy of venturing into new areas in your life and increasing that joy by spreading it to others in any way that you choose.

You are giving me a headache. I think I will have to stop for tonight.

I do not give headaches to people, but since you are giving one to yourself it is best if we stop for now. Goodnight. Sleep well and remember that I am you.

You mean remember that you are with me, don't you?

I meant what I said. I am you. Remember this while you sleep tonight.

I did go to sleep remembering the words I am you, but I was a little puzzled by them. Once again, Grandmother had shaken my core belief system. It took several days for me to feel comfortable enough to sit down and talk to her again. Finally, I could wait no longer and I went to the computer to see if she would be there for me.

Conversation Four

Hello again, Grandmother. It has been a couple of days since we talked.

You mean, it has been a couple of days since you listened.

Yes, I guess that's true. I was busy with tedious things that I felt needed to be attended to.

Why do you feel that we cannot talk unless you are seated at the computer?

I suppose because I am afraid that if you talk to me at other times, I will not remember what you say and then I cannot write it down. I feel the need to write it down so that I can remember the things you tell me and then I can go back and read them over again to myself.

Checking out the validity of the things you hear me say?

I guess so, in a way, yes. I am still having trouble believing that I am not just making this up as I go along. When I go back and read them over to myself, then I think that sounds too smart, or too complicated! I couldn't have made this up!

Okay, if that makes you more comfortable it is fine. But as I told you previously, if you are in fact, making this up, why would that be so horrible? Do you plan to use this information to harm anyone? Are you making things up to tell people in order to confuse them? Do you plan on making a lot of money by making things up and telling others?

No, you know I am not doing that.

Of course I know you are not doing that! Why don't _you_ know that you're not doing that? Are you not instead searching for the truth and looking for answers to your questions? There is nothing bad about that. Did you know that you couldn't make anything up that is not true, because if you believe it, it becomes your truth?

But couldn't I make up lies if I wanted to? I don't want to, I'm just asking.

You can create anything you desire from your imagination. Anything that you can imagine, you can have, if you have the intention to make it come true. Everything already exists in that invisible space of intention, or the Field of Plenty, as your ancestors called it. So if everything exits, then nothing that you create can be a lie. If you imagine it as true, then it becomes your truth. You can even call it into physical form with the power of your intention and the power of your imagination. So if you are thinking this is only your imagination, you are correct in the purest sense of that word. Look up the word imagination in your dictionary.

I did Grandmother and I am amazed at the actual meaning of the word. It does not mean what I have always thought it meant. Webster says; _the act, process, or power of forming a mental picture of something not present, and especially of something one has not known or experienced._ It also says; _creative ability and a creation of the mind. The verb to imagine says to form a mental picture, or to think of._ That means that I use my imagination all of the time and over time I think of something, I am imagining it, right? I am making an image of it in my mind so that I can see it! I imagine everything! I am just imagining this conversation with you, aren't I? Get it? It was a joke.

I get it, as you say, but it really isn't a joke, it is the truth. You do imagine everything. You have imagined everything that you have and you could imagine everything that you ever wanted to have. And once you have imagined or imaged it in your mind, you can then bring it into the physical plane of reality by the power of your intent. You can bring it into the form of matter. If it matters, then it *is* matter. If it has to become matter to matter, does it matter? It's up to you and your imagination! Get it? It's kind of a joke.

I'm getting another headache. And yes, I get it. Sort of anyway. Can't you speak in a way that is not so complicated? We're not all rocket scientists you know. No offense intended, Grandmother.

None taken, child. You cannot offend me. Let me try to explain it in a simpler manner. Everything that has taken on form in this physical realm has become matter. It has manifested from the higher plane of spirit and taken on a denser vibration. It matters or becomes matter in order to be seen on this plane. If you can't see it yet, it has not mattered or it has not become matter. If it *doesn't* matter, then it *isn't* matter. Do you see that? That does not mean that it doesn't exist, just that it hasn't manifested in this realm of matter. Is that easier?

A little bit, thank you. So I can cause a thing to matter by imagining it into form on this plane, correct?

Yes, by the power of your intent. Would you like to talk about your intent?

I'm not sure. Will it be as confusing as mattering and imagining?

Hopefully not. (Smile) Your intent is the power that brings your imaginings into the realm of matter. Your imagination matters! (I couldn't resist).

You make me smile Grandmother, but what if people wanted to imagine all kinds of horrible things and make them real, and then by their intentions did that?

You mean horrible things like war, famine, rape, murder, poverty and prejudice? It appears that someone has already done that. A lot of someone's have done just that. It takes a lot of intent and a lot of imaginings to bring horrors like those into physical reality on such a global scale. But you can begin to imagine love, peace, plenty, and healing. And one by one people can change what matters on the planet. You can change what becomes "matter" and manifests into the physical plane of your reality. Are you willing to try and do that?

Yes, I am willing to try. But you will have to help me.

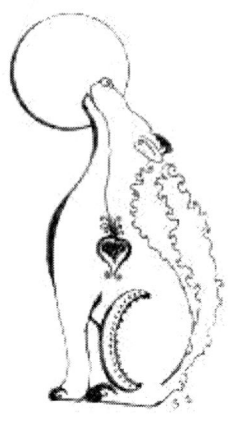

Summer 2006   July

For the past week or so, I had been focused on attending a Fire Walk that was taking place at a retreat center close by. I was nervous about attending and a bit skeptical, but was also fascinated by the prospect of actually doing it. It turned out to be one of the most empowering things I have ever done. I hadn't made time to sit and talk with Grandmother before I went to the Fire Walk, so I was excited and anxious to talk with her about the experience. Of course, when I went to her, she was waiting patiently for me.

Conversation Five

Aho Grandmother. I have been hearing you talk to me, but I haven't sat down at the computer to type out the things you are saying. A lot has happened since I last did that. I went to the Fire Walk and I walked on fire!! I feel like a completely different person than I was before I went to the Fire Walk.

And so you are, child. You learned much and you have done well. My heart swells with pride and love for you and for the things that you have allowed yourself to experience. I was there and I saw everything. Of course, you know that because you felt me very close and very real, did you not? Do you understand more that I am you and you are me? We walked the fire together as we do all things together. You are an individual yes, but you are not separate from anything that exits. You are one with Me, the Earth, the stars, the plants, the animals, the rainbows, the planets, the oceans, the rocks and

mountains and every other being in this world and all the other worlds as well.

I was one with the fire when I walked on the coals wasn't I? That's why it didn't burn me, why would it burn itself, right? Also, it became an illusion; the fire was not real to me. I entered a different dimension where the fire did not exist, didn't I?

Yes, you did. The fire did not matter to you, did it?

No, it didn't and it was an awesome feeling! But Grandmother, even though the Fire Walk was so awesome, I have had a difficult lesson to learn since then. I was really hurt and disappointed by a friend. Something that I had looked forward to, turned out not to be what I was expecting.

Ah yes, your expectations. You are learning to enter every situation with less and less expectation, aren't you? You were disappointed with the way things occurred, but you still learned a valuable lesson. Things just ARE. Things are not good or bad, they just ARE. It is what you do with the experience inside of yourself that makes it one way or the other for you, do you understand? You also have finally heard the message that has been coming to you for a long time now. You are enough. You do not need another person to carry you, or to make you worthy. You are enough. Now you will move forward at a much more rapid pace. The vision that I have given you or that you have created for your self, which is the same thing, will begin to matter for you. It is going to come into view in this dimension if you choose to make it matter. The leadings you are getting are true and real, so do not be fearful of heeding them, Firewalker!

There is much work to be done in this period of time and in this space of history. Everyone who is becoming enlightened must share with others the opportunity to become enlightened so that as many people as choose to will be ready for the great changes that are to occur. It will be a beautiful time, and a very important time in the history of the planet Earth, but it will also be difficult. As a mother, you know that birth, though beautiful, is difficult, messy, painful, and oftentimes traumatic. The rebirth of your planet will be all of those things and more. You must be totally connected to Source and completely trust who you know yourself to be. The change will be quite overwhelming for many people and many souls will choose not to stay. This is okay. But for the ones who do stay, there will be work ahead for all of them. Important and powerful spiritual work. Different people will have different kinds of work to do. Some will till the soil; some will work with herbs and plants, the basic skills of staying alive kind of work. Do not fret yourself about learning many different new things. There is not time for that. Learn what you can, of course, but your focus is to be spiritual work. And the knowledge that you require for any type of work is already programmed into your brain and is implanted in your heart and soul. Hear this: You will be able to do whatever is needed when the situation arises. Did you hear me? Any knowledge that you need will be provided for you whether you have studied it or not, whenever you need it. All you have to do is receive it. This is a future occurrence, not an immediate happening. Although you experience flashes of it now, which you call intuition. Intuition is simply tapping into that vast store of knowledge that is accessible to anyone who will be open enough to receive it. Intuition, as you know means to know something without mental effort. So it is. When you set aside your mental efforts and receive information directly through your spirit, you will know what needs to be done and how to do it.

Grandmother, sometimes when I hear of how things will be during that time, I feel afraid. I used to feel that way when I heard about the Rapture in church and I found some comfort in thinking that Jesus would take care of me. Now you're telling me that the fear I felt as a child was well founded, that things will be very bad just like the church predicted!

No, I am telling you that things will be difficult, and that you will have to be very connected to your soul and to the Source and to all things in order to survive. I also told you that some souls will choose not to stay here for that period. The church told you that only the good people would leave with Jesus and that the sinners would be left behind to suffer. You may choose to leave at any time, or you may choose to stay, and help bring in a new period in Earth's history. Either way you choose is good. Do you see the difference? The church said those left behind would be doomed to live here on Earth with the devil in control. I am telling you that there is no devil, save the one of your own making. It will be an era of much change. This is not God's punishment for the Earth, or Judgment Day for all mankind. It is a time of tremendous changes and shifts in the Earth's energies. A new world will be born, just as the Bible and many other holy texts and prophecies have foretold. Your Earth Mother will groan with birth pangs and many natural disasters will occur. You have seen the beginning of the changes already in the drastic weather patterns around the world, global warming, earthquakes and the like. Hear this child; these are not times to fear. These are times of rejoicing, for mankind is approaching the pinnacle of its history. A story that began millions of years ago is coming to its climactic conclusion.

A leap in the spiritual evolution of humankind is taking place and will signal the beginning of an age of peace and harmony such as has never been seen before.

Humans and other beings from the far reaches of the universe will join hands and remember that they are One and that they have sprung from the same Source and that they share the same destiny. That destiny is to live in harmony with all that exits, to join energy with all beings and to live as you were intended to live. The life you were meant to live is one of love, light, harmony, peace, and joy. You are creative light-filled, love-energy that has taken on physical form for a specific span of time. That span of time is almost over for all human beings. In fact, time itself, as you experience it is almost over. Do not fret yourself over the death of loved ones. There is no death; there is only a change of form. I am telling you that in a relatively short time you will be able to take any form that you wish, at any time that you wish. The Earth changes will be of such magnitude on all planes of existence, that you will be able to reach your loved ones that have already changed forms whenever you desire to do so. Child, I can see that you are tired, and feeling a bit overwhelmed with this information. Get rested, dear one, for we have much to do. I love you.

Grandmother, I love you too. If I am making you up, then I hope I don't stop because you bring me much joy. Thank you.

And you bring me much joy also. We are reflections of each other's joy. Sleep well, and remember I am you.

Conversation Six

Good morning, Grandmother. I woke up feeling a bit depressed this morning and I don't know why. But I look forward to your lessons for today.

You feel depressed, as you put it, because of the many emotions churning around inside of you. You have yet to learn fully how to accept these emotions and then let them pass through your body and be gone. It is okay to feel sadness, grief, loss and any other emotion. You must realize that these emotions are purely energy and do not have to linger in your body. I am not telling you to suppress your feelings, I am telling you to feel them and then let them go!

Remember how fear manifested itself in your physical body at the Fire Walk? You felt it, shook it off, literally shook it out of your body and then you walked on fire. There will come a day when you can shake off any feeling that you do not want to have. Then you can open yourself completely to the energies of love, peace, joy and light. These are the things that you are. You don't have to just feel joyful, you are joy. The same with love, peace, light and all the other positive energies. These energies are what you are made of. God is Love. That's what the Bible taught you as a child, correct? Well, if God is Love, and you are God, what does that make you? If God is light, peace, harmony, laughter and Oneness, what does that make you? Remember I told you that we are reflections of each other's joy? More accurately we are reflections of each other, because joy is who we are. When you see Me, you look into a mirror and see the reflection of your self; you are the joy that you see. Likewise, when I look at you, I see a reflection of the joy that I am, because you are the mirror of Myself. Do you understand?

I think so, Grandmother. All I have to do to stay in a place of joy, is to continually look at you?

All you have to do to BE joy, is to continue to see yourself as Me. You don't have to look at, or look to, anyone else to see who you really are. All you need to do is to look inside of yourself and see that God is there. You are God and God is you. You need to hear this over and over because it is a foreign idea to you. You still tend to think in terms of God being somewhere outside of yourself. That makes it difficult to reach Him/Her when you wish to communicate. When you want to talk to God, talk to yourself! I will answer you because I Am you. Isn't that what you are doing right now as you type these words? You are speaking to the God inside of you and God is answering you. Your internal dialogue is always a talk with God. That is how one can pray without ceasing. You could not be down on your knees or lighting candles without ceasing in order to pray, could you? How would you ever do anything else? You couldn't. Ceaseless prayer is a constant communion with the God who resides inside of you, because it IS you. Did you realize that every thought that goes through your mind is the thought of God? When you wonder what God wants you to do all you need to do is ask, what do I want to do? And you will have the answer. Whatever you want to do is what God wants. It is as simple as that. God does not want you to suffer or sacrifice, or beat yourself up in order to please Him/Her.

A few weeks passed. Hurricane Katrina hit Louisiana and caused massive widespread destruction. This tragedy affected me greatly and I was feeling depressed. I could feel the pain of the victims. The television news constantly played images that were heart wrenching and fear producing. Finally I took my concerns to Grandmother.

Conversation Seven

Grandmother, I greet you with respect and love.

I greet you with the same, child. And how are you?

You know how I am Grandmother. I am tired and depressed and a little bit scared. This tragedy in Louisiana has me feeling very angry and upset. I have had a feeling for weeks that something bad was going to happen. Is this what I was feeling?

Indeed, this is what you were psychically picking up on, child. The thought waves or intent if you will, were put into place months ago for this to happen. It is the result of collective thought forms that have been made into matter by billions of people. You will find yourself becoming more and more sensitive, as will many people. You will find yourself picking up the thought waves of others. This comes with spiritual growth and is part of the process of The Awakening. It can be a tremendous aid to you. It can also become a great burden if you allow it to be so. You must learn how to sense these thought waves and send healing energy to wherever they are emanating from. Never keep them in your own body or mind, or they can make you physically ill. As soon

as you sense a thought wave that feels negative to you, pray and send light and love to the place of origin. If you do not know where it is originating from, just send it out into the universe, as the energy knows where to go. Then RELEASE it and do not hold it in yourself in any way. This is how one learns to walk with one foot in each realm. You can learn how to release energy immediately and not let it affect you. Do not worry that you will be unfeeling or uncaring. Learning how to send positive energy and how to release negative energy is the most loving, caring thing you can do for people in crisis. Your feelings of sadness and concern may be commendable, but they serve no purpose. Do you understand?

You can care about people and the things that happen, and still be able to detach yourself from the negative impact of feeling them. It is only in this way that you can have any effect on the *bad* things that occur in your world. Crying, feeling sorry and being depressed only adds to the collective thought wave of destruction. Remember that when you begin to feel these emotions. Then, immediately adjust your energy field to one of love, light, hope and goodness. Yes, you can make a difference. The transformation is going to occur child, and that is a fact. But you can help make it an easier transformation. Natural disasters are a part of what the Earth is going to experience and often natural disasters kill people. But you have to remember that death is only an illusion. This time of Change is a mere wisp in the scheme of eternity. You must learn how to look outside of time, as you know and experience it, in the physical world. We will work on this together another time.

The idea of learning how to look outside of time intrigued me very much. Time travel and all that it implies has captivated my imagination since I was a child. I read The Time Machine and never considered it to be science fiction. I totally believed it, so I could hardly wait for the next day to come. When it did, I sat down at the computer and jumped right into the conversation.

Conversation Eight

Okay, Grandmother, how are we going to work on me experiencing time in a different way?

Here is an example of how time really works. It flows along like a river, if you will. You can step into that river at any point. You can enter it at one point and be where you were ten or twenty years ago. You can enter it at another point and be ten or twenty years ahead of where you are now. The river of time is flowing along smoothly, endlessly and continuously. There are no breaks or sections in it. If you stand outside of it, you can choose where you wish to enter. When you are in the river and measuring it by days, months, or years, you are only aware of the particular point where you are standing. When you step out of the river, which is to say outside of the human definition of time measurements, you can stand on the banks, so to speak and see the whole river. Or at least see that it flows onward with no end in sight. Then you can choose where you wish to enter. You can walk

downstream or upstream to any point in your past, or future, life. The river keeps flowing and does not stop. If you enter in your past, your future is still flowing, as is your present. It all exists simultaneously but you are generally aware of only the part where you are standing, or living. Let me put it this way . . . your past, present and future is happening now. In retrospect, the years gone by seem to be very short, yet while you were experiencing them, they may have felt endless, right? I am telling you that all of time, when viewed from the perspective of eternity, feels like that. Try and grasp the enormity of what timeless time is. If you hear someone say that time is running out, know that this is not possible. Time never can and never will, run out. It cannot, because time doesn't really exist. It is an illusion (one of many in the third dimension). There is only one enormous NOW and when tomorrow arrives, that will be the NOW you are in. When you begin to experience your life as NOW, then your lesson of timelessness will be learned. I do understand that deadlines, schedules and such are necessary right now for those of you in the third dimension. But soon people will be working more and more outside of the realm of normal time.

Grandmother, I am giving myself a headache again. It feels sometimes like you are physically stretching my brain! The things that you tell me seem so weird and hard to understand sometimes. I worry that I am going crazy, or having hallucinations, or that I'm just plain making things up to impress people.

And how many people have you impressed so far with the information I have shared with you?

Well, I've read some of your messages to a few friends and family members and to my husband. They seemed impressed.

And what have you gained from impressing all these people?

Nothing, I guess. Except the feeling that maybe I am not crazy after all. And that I might really have something important to share with people.

Is that a bad thing?

No, I suppose it's not. Really, I guess when you think about it, it's a good thing.

So your so-called hallucinations have actually helped you feel better about yourself and maybe enlightened a few other people as well? I think, then, that it is a very good thing, don't you?

Yes, Grandmother, now I do. And I'll say it again . . . if I am just making you up, then let me continue to do so, because you bring me much joy.

And you bring joy to me also. I needn't let you do anything. You can do anything you choose to do for as long as you choose to do it. I hope you choose to continue our relationship because I have much I want to teach you.

I do choose to do that, Grandmother. But I have to stop for now because my brain hurts! That's because you're stretching it, right?

Indeed, I am child, quite literally in fact. That is the source of some of your headaches. The rest are a result of you thinking too much! Rest now, I will be here when you are ready to proceed.

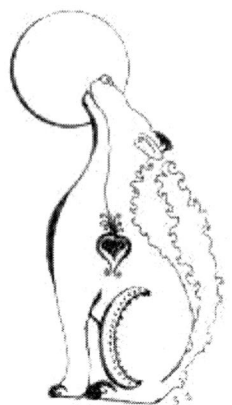

August 2005

Conversation Nine

Aho, Grandmother. Well, let's see what has been going on since the last time we talked. Oh, I know! I had a booth at the Intuitive Arts Fair over the weekend.

So you did, child. Were you pleased with the day?

Yes, I was, Grandmother. I could have made a little more money, but that wasn't the purpose, was it?

No it was not.

The purpose was for you to see how powerful you are and how much you can accomplish, even if you have to do it by yourself as you say. You drew people to your booth with your own energy and did not depend on someone else to attract them for you. It was meant for your friend not to show up so that you could see this in action.

It is good to have friends and helpers, but do not ever again depend on someone else to do for you what you can do for yourself. And I am speaking of

doing your own thing energetically, not physically. Every person's energy is unique and all their own. You have work to do, as does everyone, and only you can do it. People's intuitive abilities will begin to increase tenfold in a very short span of time. You must all be ready to receive the information that will be coming through to you. It is highly spiritual work that you have been chosen to do and are being prepared for, child. I know that you do not feel worthy, but that is your own fear speaking to you, not Me. You are worthy, as all people are worthy, of gifts to be used for the purpose of healing. Indeed, all people do have a gift, but not all people choose to use it or develop it.

At this time in history, especially, it is vitally important for each person to find and develop and begin to use their particular gift for the healing of the Universe. That is the purpose of these expanded abilities. It is not to impress others, or to be a sideshow for people to come and marvel at. It is expressly for the purpose of healing your planet that so many new abilities are being exhibited by enlightened beings on your Earth.

You have chosen, as has everyone, to incarnate at this point in Earth's history. Therefore, it follows that you have a plan and a purpose for being here, does it not? Let your soul lead you in the work you do. Don't be afraid to charge for the services you provide, but do not let money be your primary end or goal. I promise you child, that you will never go hungry or have unpaid bills. Remember that your intent can make anything matter and that refers to money also. Money is merely energy in one of its forms. It only has as much power as you give it. Remember that everything is energy and you can bring anything into form with your intent. You are not meant to serve money. It was created to serve you.

(Next day)

Conversation Ten

Good morning, Grandmother. I greet you with joy in my heart.

Good morning, child. I greet you in the same manner. What do you wish to speak of today?

Well, I am going to teach my first Reiki class this weekend, and I am a little bit nervous. Can you help me with that?

With being nervous, or with teaching?

With both, actually! Can you?

Of course I can. First, being nervous is fine; it will help to keep you humble. Never feel like you have all the answers, even though you do.

Grandmother, with all due respect, that doesn't make any sense. If I have all the answers, why can't I feel like I do?

Because they have yet to be discovered within you. The answers to all your questions lie within your own self, so you have them, but you haven't accessed them. Do you see the difference?

I think so. I have the possibility of knowing all the answers, is that it?

That is indeed it. All you will ever need to know, or desire to know, is hidden within your spirit. As you grow and evolve, the knowledge will become more and more apparent to you. As your mind and spirit

grow and expand, so too will the knowledge inside of them. The knowledge that you need to heal and to spread love and light, will grow ever brighter and larger. Know that what you need to teach Reiki is there. And all you have to do is share with an open heart and a desire to heal, with the intent to make it so. Do not focus on methods or modalities. Focus, instead on intent. Let your intent be to pass the attunements, to share the benefits and stress the importance of doing any healing work from a place of love and light. This is true for any teacher. If you accomplish these three things, you will have done very well. What the student does with what you give them is not your concern. Do, however, be discerning in who you choose to teach. Everyone is entitled to the knowledge, but not everyone is supposed to receive it from you. This is for your protection. No fear involved, just be aware that some individuals should not be in your energetic space at this time. You are still learning about your own boundaries, your talents and gifts. It is a time of transition for you. This is a special time of exploration, joy and discovery. It is also a spiritually vulnerable time, so use your wisdom to guide you in the choices you make. Not just concerning Reiki, but in all of your life choices.

I see that the word vulnerable has aroused the emotion of fear in you. Let me make it clearer. I am not speaking of demonic oppression, or possession, or anything demonic at all. I am saying that some circumstances might make you more open to sickness, or emotional pain. You could be put into a situation where you become enmeshed with someone else's fears or problems and this could result in pain when you try to extricate yourself from them. This can cause pain for you and for the other person. Remember that everyone is on the path of his or her choice. Not all are on the same path. No one path is better than any other; they are simply different ways of getting to the same place. Some paths, although different, can be walked harmoniously with another. Some cannot.

September 2005

Grandmother talks to me all the time, no matter where I am or what I am doing. It's a continuous internal dialogue that is always going on inside my head. Some folks might find this distracting but I am used to it, so it doesn't bother me. However, I did find it easier to focus in on her voice when I sat down at the computer. The preparation was quite simple actually. I would merely sit down, center myself and say something like, "Hello Grandmother, here I am. What do you want to talk about today?" So that's what I did this morning.

Conversation Eleven

Aho, Grandmother. I have missed talking to you. I know that you speak to me everyday, but it seems to be easier for me to hear you when I sit at the computer.

Greetings, child. Ah yes, the computer. You insist on letting this be the avenue by which we communicate. So be it, for now anyway. What is on your mind today?

I feel sad and depressed. I'm embarrassed to say that again. I seem to feel depressed a lot of the time, don't I? I might be catching a cold and it is time for my moon cycle. Even though that cycle is finished I still have the emotions that came along with it. But it feels deeper than that.

I feel sadness about so many things and they don't seem to be connected. It's like everything I've ever felt sad about came to the surface today. I feel bad about myself and the way I look. I feel old and like I don't have many years left to do something with my life. That makes me feel like not even trying to grow and learn new things. What is wrong with me?

Nothing is wrong with you, child. Old issues are being brought up in order to be cleared out so that you can receive a new and deeper surge of power. Old stuff must be cleaned out before new stuff can be put in. All is as it should be and you are just fine. You have already done much healing work on yourself, and it is time to remove the remaining blocks to your spiritual advancement. As overwhelming as it feels, the things that remain are small in quantity, and in quality. Indeed, these feelings come and go very quickly, do they not? Something that would have kept you depressed for weeks or months long ago, now comes and goes in a matter of days or even hours. Is this not true? Spirit is cleaning you out to be a channel. Trust that all happens for a good and divinely planned reason. This is a process everyone must go through. You are right square in the middle of where you need to be! Do not fight the feelings that come up. Do not try to analyze or even understand them. Simply feel them and when you are done, let them go. It really is as simple as it sounds. What makes it complicated is when you try to figure out why you feel this way. The reason why does not matter anymore. In therapy, the why is important in order to find different ways to respond to situations. This wave of emotion that you are in now is a spiritual cleansing that is necessary for you to continue on the path of evolution to a higher place of being. It too, will pass, child. Do not fret or be discouraged. This is not a chemical imbalance, nor is it hormonal. Those things may come into play and make it more intense, but they are not the cause.

This is a divinely planned and ordered state of emotional imbalance.

An ordered state of imbalance?

Yes, it is needed so that your emotions can be fully balanced, and you can be in harmony with the purpose for which you have come to the Earth. You have as yet, just a mere glimpse of what is in store for you. You have a wonderful purpose and a healing to bring to the Earth. Everyone does. Everyone who is here *now* has a specific plan that they came to carry out. Do not compare yourself with others. Do not feel inferior, or superior. All beings on Earth at this time have chosen to be here for the great Shift that is coming and indeed has already started.

Work together with your brothers and sisters who are also striving to heal themselves and bring awareness to those still in the dark. Recognize what a great blessing all your teachings have been to you and avail yourself of all the light and knowledge that is accessible to you. Pray over each teaching and see if it resonates with your heart and spirit. If it does, then draw it to you and use it. If it does not, then discard it and do not linger or wonder about it. Your truth is your truth. Someone else's truth may not be yours. But there is one truth that is universal and the same for everyone . . . God is Love. You are God, therefore you are love. Love is all there is. God is all there is and nothing that you do in love will ever be in vain.

October 2005

Conversation Twelve

Hello Grandmother. I have missed you. I can't believe that I still have a lingering fear of sitting down and talking to you.

Hello, child. Why are you scared to come to Me? Am I so frightening?

No, Grandmother. It's not you that scares me, it's me! I am afraid that when I do come to hear from you that you won't speak, or that I won't be able to hear you, or that old favorite of mine . . . that I will just make something up out of my own longing.

Child, I am always speaking to you. Hearing me is your choice and we have talked at length about making things up, have we not? Let me tell you a truth. Your desire for God is your deepest assurance that God exists. If God was nonexistent, you could not feel a longing to find Him/Her. But you continue to look outside of yourself for God, and God is IN YOU. You believe this, but you do not yet know it. When you *know* it you will feel the peace that you yearn for. When you are afraid of doing something bad or wrong, know that these feelings are just hang ups from your past, residual fear from your religious upbringing. Exploring other spiritual paths will help to dissolve those lingering fears. Just like exploring the Native American path did. Every time you explore something new and different from what you are used to, it helps to rid you of those last few fears that remain. As you study and realize that there truly

is more than one way to God, you will become more comfortable with your own changing beliefs. And don't think that you will find just the one way that is right for you, because each path has a piece of the whole truth. Feel free to explore and study and find out which piece of the Truth feels right to you and for you. Each person's path is unique and individual. It is alright to affiliate yourself with a particular denomination or set of beliefs, if you choose to do so. And there are good reasons to do this, not the least of which is a sense of community. But be careful that you do not get caught up in a set of rules and regulations. Structure is one thing, inflexibility is another. And flexible is one thing that God surely is! Flexible, changing, (not in character, just in manifestation!) always moving and expanding. If you wish to know God IN YOU, you must have these characteristics also. Putting God in a box, as people say, is what you do because you think He/She is too big for you to know intimately. You are more comfortable with a concept of God that is small enough for you to handle. You keep God in that box even after you realize that God is in you and that is because you do not remember how big YOU are. You are big enough to have God in you, because you are as big as God is. In fact, you are God. How does that make your lingering Baptist feel? (Soft laugh)

Frankly, Grandmother, that makes my lingering Baptist more than just a little afraid. It feels so egotistical and full of pride to say that I am God. I thought we were supposed to fight against ego and strive to be humble and not think too much of ourselves?

Who told you that?

The Baptists.

That figures. Now, first of all, anything that you fight against, or strive for, will just get bigger! The more attention you give it, the more energy you are sending to it and the more power you give it. If you want to get rid of your ego (which by the way you never will . . . no one can) then just ignore it. (It can be made less controlling) Strive to be humble? No! Just don't think about it. Strive is an awful word, by the way. Go look up the word strive, child.

I did Grandmother. It means; *to carry on a conflict or effort; to try hard to win; or to content with.*

I know. I told you it wasn't a good word, or perhaps an inappropriate word is a better way to describe it. Do you want conflict and contention to be a part of your relationship with God? You don't have to try to win, you have already won. In fact, there was never a competition. Here is your word for the day . . . are you ready? RELAX. This is your word to meditate on for now. It is a good word for any of you to meditate on. Most of you put too much pressure on yourselves and stress yourself out when it comes to your relationship with God. This is totally unnecessary. A relationship with God is easy, natural and simple.

Thank you, Grandmother. I will meditate on this word as you asked.

My love for you knows no bounds, child.

And neither does mine for you, Grandmother.

Conversation Thirteen

Good morning, Grandmother, I have a question. I was thinking about what you said about the ego. You said it cannot be gotten rid of, but only can be controlled and therefore lessened, right?

That is correct, child. That is what I said.

I have always been taught that ego was the part of us that went against God and wanted only our own selfish will. In fact, I have heard it said that EGO equals "easing God out!" I was taught that ego is the mask we wear that covers who we really are in our divinity. And that ego starts when we are born and is made up of others' expectations of us as to who and what we could be. Can you tell me some more about the ego?

Certainly, child. First of all, there is no part of you that is not God. As your Native American teaching tells you nothing is outside of the lodge of Creator, nothing. That includes ego. Consider this. If you are all God (and you all are), then no part of you is not God. Ego is tricky because it can try to control you, along with your desires and actions. Just because something's in Creator's lodge (and everything is), doesn't necessarily mean it is something you want to dominate your life. In fact, you don't want anything to dominate your life except Divine Love. And perhaps encompass is a better word than dominate. Ego is, indeed, something that forms after you incarnate into a flesh body. It is a part of your mind, or human brain, if you will. It is necessary for you to

have ego to function in the flesh. Your spirit self has nothing except Spirit, consciousness, love, light, and joy. In order to deal with life in the third dimension, ego is formed. You might say that ego is the survival part of the human brain. Survival is good, unless it becomes a matter of survival of the fittest, or strongest. Then again you have competition. Ego is what competes with others for survival. The lie is that competition even exits. It does not. Everyone is equally important and valuable. You do not have to compete for God's love or approval. This is what makes for all the separate religions and denominations. Each one believes that they have found the only way to being God's chosen. People through the ages have fought bloody wars over these ideas, actually being willing to kill others to prove that they are more loved by God than anyone else!

It really is very sad and very ignorant, isn't it Grandmother?

Indeed it is, child, indeed it is.

Grandmother, I would like to keep writing down the things you tell me so that I won't forget them and so that perhaps one day I might share them with others. Would that be okay for me to do?

Now why do you ask me permission to do what your heart tells you to do? Haven't I always told you that whatever your will is, that is My will for you? My desires are your desires.

Yes, Grandmother, you have told me that. I guess I still haven't fully grasped that I can do whatever I wish without bringing down the wrath of God on my head! Tell me again why I don't have to worry about displeasing You or making You angry by doing the wrong thing.

It is because I AM YOU and YOU ARE ME. Whatever your will is, then that is My will also. If you desire to be happy and prosperous, then I desire for you to be happy and prosperous. If you desire to be poor and depressed, then I desire for you to be poor and depressed.

EXCUSE ME?? You just said you want me to be poor and depressed! What kind of thing is that for God to say??

No child. I said IF that is what you desire, then that is also what I desire. How could it be any different if our desires are the same? That is why it is so important for you to connect with your desires and to be sure that they are your true desires. And don't forget that your beliefs about yourself and what you deserve come into play too. You may think that you desire something, but on an energetic level don't feel that you deserve it. Since God (you and Me) operates on an energetic level, that, then, is the true desire even though you might be unaware of it. So if your desires are not manifesting, examine your energetic beliefs.

I think I am beginning to really understand that, Grandmother. May I ask you another question?

Certainly. If that is what you desire to do (Smile).

Very funny, Grandmother. Okay, well, I am going to meet with a Cherokee elder and maybe begin to study with this person. Is this my next teacher that I have been waiting for?

You know what they say . . . When the student is ready, the teacher will appear. Are you ready?

Yes, I think I am.

You think you are, or you are? There is a difference, you know. Your brain thinks that you are. Your Spirit knows that you are. So which is it? You think or you know?

I know that I am ready, Grandmother. I feel a sense of excitement and anticipation when I think about being able to study with this elder. It feels right. But I also can't believe that this is happening to me. I guess energetically, I feel like I don't deserve to have this wonderful opportunity. How can I feel both of those emotions at the same time? Is it because one of them is deeper, on an energetic level, than the other?

Yes, child. You still struggle with your own sense of self-worth. But you are getting so much better at knowing who you really are. And this elder will also know if this is supposed to take place. You truly desire to have this teacher in your life and your awareness of the energetic level and its effects, help you to manifest your desires. In other words, you are *aware* that you feel unworthy. You are also aware that this unworthiness is no longer your truth. Through this awareness, you are making new pathways in your energy body that conform to the truth of who you are, what you are capable of and what you deserve. Begin to express gratitude for the opportunity to study with this new teacher. She has much to show you and to tell you. And do stop feeling disloyal to your previous teacher! There are many teachers in each of your lives.

Thank you, Grandmother. I have to leave now, and go visit my mother.

Bless you, child.

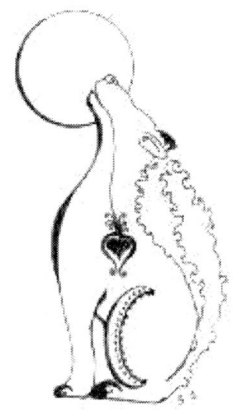

December 2006

My mother was very ill during this time and I went to visit her as often as I could. That, along with regular every day responsibilities, kept me from sitting with Grandmother as much as I would have liked. But as always, She was right there when I finally did make time to sit and listen to her.

Conversation Fourteen

Greetings, Grandmother. Too much time has passed since I sat down to talk with you. I will try to do better and meet with you every day. I have something troubling me and I would like to ask you about it, if that is okay?

That is why I am here. To answer your questions.

Okay, thank you. Recently, I met a person who says they channel information from another realm and communicate with the dead. But the messages that they bring do not ring true to me. I don't mean I think this person is evil, or trying to deliberately mislead people, but something about it doesn't feel right.

Yes? And what is your question?

I guess its how do I discern what is true and what isn't, without judging someone else? And what do I do with the information when I perceive that someone is not really hearing from Spirit?

First of all, you discern that something is not true for you just the way you already have discerned that this

person's message is not for you. You feel or sense that it is not your truth. You do not judge whether it is right or wrong, you just know that it is not relevant to your life at this time. And what do you do with that information? Nothing. There is nothing that needs to be done with it, or about it. You have had your own discernment, now you let it be. Everyone else who comes into contact with this person will have to have their own discernment about the information that is being offered. Perhaps for someone else it will be true and will be just what they need to hear at a specific time in their life. It might be their truth, even though it is not yours. Do you understand this?

Sort of, I guess. But this thing about everyone having their own truth and how it can be different for each person is still kind of hard for me to grasp. I want truth to be a solid unchanging fact that I can depend on. Otherwise how do I measure anything in my life? How do I judge the certainty of anything? Any experience, or information, or any emotion I feel?

You do not need to measure them, child. Just let them happen. Then chose how you will respond to each experience, choose how you will use any information, what you will do with each emotion and choose how you will grow from every experience also. The one unchanging truth is this: Everything is constantly changing.

Even God, Great Spirit, Creator??

Yes, even all of those (and they are one and the same as you know). But the fact that they change does not make them untrustworthy. That's where you get stuck.

I do get stuck there, Grandmother. To think that there is no unchanging truth, nothing stable to hold on to makes me nervous. And it does feel untrustworthy and unsafe. Sort of confusing too.

I have told you before, child, that God is always changing in manifestation, but NOT in character. God Is, Was and Always Shall Be. God is love, light, joy and peace. God is never ending, always creating and always moving and changing in form, but never in character. How God manifests to people and how they choose to find God is their own personal choice. No way is right or wrong, or better than another. The Baptists have their truth, the Methodists have their truth. The Catholics have their truth and so on. So truth in these instances is different for each person depending on what they were brought up to believe. Each one has their own truth that may be different from yours. But the GOD that each person or group is reaching for and trying to find, is the same. There is only one God and that God is all there is. That Truth is unchanging.

Thank you, Grandmother. If I may, could I return to this discussion about truth at another time? I have questions about something else that is pressing on my mind.

Your wish is my command.

I get it. Like the genie in the bottle, right? You can be so funny, Grandmother.

Life can be funny, child. Now what are these pressing questions about?

Well, I am teaching a class on the Medicine Wheel at my Friday morning group and I am a little bit anxious. Could you please give me your thoughts on the Medicine Wheel?

Of course, child. Do not be nervous. Just enter sacred space with an open heart and the words will be given to you. You cannot fail me or disappoint me. Neither do you represent me, so put these frets to rest. You are me, and I am you in the manifested form that appears as Laughing Heart to others. We will simply share what we have learned about the Medicine Wheel, together. The Medicine Wheel is LIFE. It is holy and it is all of creation. On one level, it is a symbol of the year and the twelve seasons through which all of creation moves in a circular fashion. But it is much more than that. It is the seasons of your life and the cycles of birth and rebirth that every soul experiences. It is creation itself. It is love and balance and growth. It is learning and serving and healing. It is your relationship with Creator and with all your relations. It is the connectedness of all things. It is how the world was created and how Earth continues to exist. It is how all humankind was created and continues to exist. You enter the wheel on this plane at the time of your physical birth, but you have always existed within it and always will. The Medicine Wheel is the All. Everyone is inside of this wheel, no matter what they call it, or how they describe it in their own school of thought. The Medicine Wheel is the I am That I Am. It is Creator symbolized by a physical form that the human eye can see and learn the lessons of life from. Be reverent and respectful and know the space of the wheel is sacred and holy. All of life is sacred and holy. Creator has made nothing that is mundane, or unimportant. All things, all beings are loved and cherished by Creator. The first peoples knew this and that is why they took care of Mother Earth and all their relations. If the human race is to survive the changes that are coming, they must return to this way of thinking and living. Embrace the Wheel and dance in it with joy. Changes are indeed ahead, but all is as it should be. The journey around the Wheel will help you to see and understand what your part in the coming change is. It will help you know how to be most effective in accomplishing the work that you have incarnated on this planet to do. Do not fear when you hear of extreme circumstances or financial ruin and natural disasters. Know that the old must be torn down before the new can be brought into form. Keep your eyes and your hearts intentions upon the new future and not on the transition that is even now occurring. Be wise, and cautious when necessary, but do not be fearful. There is no reason to fear.

Thank you, Grandmother. Now I am off to teach the class! (but, I am still a little bit nervous!)

It was during this class that Grandmother chose to speak publicly for the very first time, much to my chagrin and surprise. I was meticulously prepared to teach on the subject of the Medicine Wheel and felt relatively confident in spite of my fears of speaking in front of people. Grandmother was quite vocal as I drove to the meeting and I couldn't concentrate on what I was planning to share with the group. Finally, in hopes of shutting her up, I said that I would be glad to share one of her messages by reading it to the group. That seemed to work. ("Seemed to" being the operative phrase here.) I arrived at the meeting. My introduction and meditation went smoothly. However, as I began to talk about the actual teachings of the Medicine Wheel a very strange thing happened. I would look at the Wheel I had made and my mind would just go blank. It happened again and again. I thought maybe it was nerves at first, but oddly enough I didn't feel nervous any more. The harder I tried to recall my planned lesson, the blanker my mind would become. All I could hear was Grandmother chattering away inside of my head. At last, in desperation, I mumbled an apology and made some sort of attempted explanation to the group. Then I closed my eyes, took a deep breath, and let Grandmother speak.

(Several days later)

Conversation Fifteen

Grandmother, please tell me what happened in group on Friday!!! I know I was prepared and I could recite the information by heart practically. But when I got in front of all those people I just went blank!! I could hear *You* talking in my head, but couldn't remember anything I had prepared to say. Was I just using you as an excuse to cover up how nervous I was and to keep from looking stupid?

No child, you did not do either of those things. I told you on your way to the group that I wanted to talk.

But I didn't know you meant talk out loud!!!

Well, that's what I meant and you honored me by letting me do so. I thank you. I will be speaking again at group and maybe in other places too if you will allow it to happen.

Grandmother, that makes me almost as anxious as speaking in front of the group did!! I am afraid that people will think I am just making you up. And what if I can't hear you when you wish to talk? Then I really would look stupid, just sitting there waiting for something to "come through" and having nothing happen!

Your main concern seems to be looking stupid in front of people. Let's put that to rest right from the start. That is ego talking. Even if you did look stupid, as you put it, what does it matter in the larger scheme of things? You must be willing to risk it if you want to make a difference in the world. I have knowledge to give people and I wish to use you as a

mouthpiece, if I may use that term. You still ask the question; "Who am I to tell people anything?" And that also comes from ego. Everyone has knowledge to share. Everyone has a gift, remember? One of your gifts is being able to stand aside and let me talk. You keep writing down all the things I share with you, but are not willing to take a chance and share with anyone else, except for a few people that are closest to you. I am telling you that the time has come to share with people in a larger way. You know that I am always gentle with you, child. I will not overtake you, or possess you in a way that makes you fearful. But if you will honor me by standing aside and putting away your pride and fear, I will begin to speak more often. Humans have received information from the spirit world in this manner for thousands of years. If other people can, why can't you?

I will try my best to stand aside Grandmother and let you speak whenever you wish to do so. How will I know when you want to?

I will tell you, child, just like I told you at your group last Friday. As you become quicker to hear me, and to stand aside as soon as you hear me speak to you inside, I will not need to blank out your thoughts to get your attention. I had to get your attention in a big way at your group since it was the first time I had ever asked to talk through you in public. Since I will be asking this of you more and more often, you will have plenty of opportunities to learn to hear me and to stand aside as soon as I ask permission to speak. I will always ask your permission because I will never override your free will. I will, however, be persistent in my asking. (Smile)

Grandmother, I felt so strange after the group when everyone was coming up to me and telling me how wonderful the presentation was. All those people were crowding around me and they wanted to speak to me and they wanted something from me because I am a Medicine Woman. I could feel the hunger in some of them. It was so strong that I could literally feel it in the air around us. It made me feel inadequate and very sad. Why was that?

It made you feel inadequate because you think that YOU have to give them something and you don't' believe that you have anything worthwhile to give. But all you have to do is share with them the things that you have learned from Me, and from your other teachers. It made you feel sad because you are sensitive, and it saddens your heart to see people that are hungry and not being fed. Do you not understand that you can help to alleviate their hunger by not being afraid to let Me speak? It is your gift to bring a message to those who are seeking for spiritual food. I, Grandmother, have a message that is important for these times. You have the ability to open yourself and let me bring that message. So, child, together we have work to do and much to accomplish. I ask that you put aside your fears and insecurities and enter a space where you have never been before. In this space, together, we will bring a message of comfort and hope to a weary world that is afraid of what is to come. The coming changes are of a nature to make one afraid, but there is no need to fear. The changes are necessary and those who are meant to get through them alive in their physical bodies will do so. Those who choose to change form and pass to the other side will do so of their own volition and there is no fear involved.

But what about the people, Grandmother, who don't know about, or believe in the changes that are coming? What will happen to the ones who are caught unaware so to speak? It still makes me think of the Rapture and all the stuff I heard in church about being left behind to live on Earth with the anti-Christ. Sometimes it still feels frightening to me and I don't like that feeling.

First of all, the people who are unaware as you say will have a choice. The changes will be so obvious that everyone will see what is happening and can choose to stay or leave. But they are not your concern, child. Creator has everything under control. Each soul will have the opportunity to leave the Earth plane, or to stay and assist in the Change. Either choice is okay. Second, if you don't like the feeling of fear, why not let it go?

That's easy for you to say, Grandmother, but it's easier said than done. It took many years for those fears to get stuck in my head, and you can't expect me to get rid of them just like that!

I don't expect you to do anything, child. I just thought that perhaps you might like to rid yourself of a feeling that you said you don't like. And frankly, we don't have years left for you to rid yourself of something that no longer serves you. The time is short and things must be brought into form more quickly than ever before. I know this is hard for you to believe, but you truly can have a desire manifested as soon as you speak it. So speak to the universe that you are not afraid of the changes to come and that you know God will be with you every step you take.

I have an idea, Grandmother. Why can't I just keep on writing down the things you tell me and then we could have a book published and lots and lots of people could read what you have to say!

Because my message needs to be heard *now*. Perhaps we will write a book later. Plus, a book is the easy way out for you at this point and I wish to stretch you. I wish for you to experience new levels of awareness and consciousness. This is a tool that will assist you in the years of change. A shift in your consciousness and a new level of AWARENESS. You have longed for and prayed for, a supernatural experience for many years and here it is. And yet you are afraid. Trust, child, that this is the answer to your prayers. Everything that has happened in your life has conspired to bring you to this very point. You are ready and it is time for you to be a channel for a message of hope and peace. I am not telling you to go on television and speak before millions. Just begin to let me speak when I ask to and we will reach the ones who need to hear the message. It may be a large group of people, or it may be just a few. Do not concern yourself with the details. I will take care of all that. Just release your fear and step into the role you have been called to walk in. Your work is not anything that you have ever imagined for yourself before. A channel for the Divine is something you would never think you could be. But that is exactly what I am telling you that you are. All beings are channels for the Divine energy. Your way to express this is by letting me speak through you. It is no better and no worse than any other way of channeling Divine energy. It is your way. Do not judge it, just be what you are.

(Next day)

Conversation Sixteen

Good morning, Grandmother. I had a very hard time last night. I tried to share with someone what You had told me and they weren't interested. I was excited and happy about the things you told me, but as soon as they ignored it, I felt very angry and I stayed angry all night. Not only that, I got mad over every little thing after that. I went to bed feeling awful.

Good morning to you too, child. I know you had a difficult night and I am sorry. But I must tell you that you brought it on yourself by needing this persons' approval in order to believe what I had told you. You caught a glimpse of what your work is here on Earth and it scared you because it felt too big. So you needed someone else's approval for you to think it was okay for you to believe it. It is time for you to stop needing and wanting the approval of anyone else. You must be strong and stand in your own truth and approve of yourself. You must realize how big and powerful you truly are. You must accept the job that is before you and embrace the changes in your own life that are occurring. Do not worry about, or seek, anyone else's approval but your own. If you recognize who and what you are, so will everyone around you. You feel sympathy and compassion for the people who come across your path and have been chosen, or agreed to be chosen let me say, to help them know who and what they are. But first you must see and believe in your own greatness. You cannot share something that you do

not have for yourself. You will teach others what you are yourself learning.

Grandmother, last night I was reading back over some of the things you have told me during the past months and years. Some of it has not come to pass. For instance, you said that I would learn from the Native American elder that I went to meet with and yet I wasn't taken on as a student.

What about this bothers you, child?

Well, to me it proves that I am just making these conversations up in my own head and they are not real, just a figment of my imagination. If they were real, then all the things that you say would happen, right?

First of all, I urge you to go back and read closely what I have told you. I think I did not say that you would be a student of this person, only that you would learn from them. And you have learned from them, have you not?

Yes, I did! I learned that some elders are still narrow minded in their thinking. They still feel the hurts that were inflicted on them by the white men and will not share their knowledge with others, unless they fit a certain criteria. I also learned that Rainbow Medicine, which is what my Medicine Woman taught me, is the path I am supposed to follow. It is not a path of one single tribe or tradition, but a blend of many. I also learned that I do not need a teacher at this point, because I am to be a teacher.

These are very good things you learned, child. Look again at the things we have discussed previously. Read with eyes that have more wisdom now and see if you can decipher what I was really telling you and what you wanted me to be telling you.

But Grandmother, if I write things that I want you to be telling me and not things that you really are telling me, then how can I ever share your words with other people? That's exactly what I have been saying scares me so much about doing this publicly! I might be just making things up that I think they want to hear! I will be a fake and a liar. I will lead people astray and be a charlatan, or whatever that word is. I don't want to do that. And now it's time for me to leave for my mom's and I am not finished talking with you. Can we talk when I get home?

Yes, child. And we can talk while you're driving to your mom's and even while you are there and on the way home too, if you wish.

Thank you, Grandmother. I know that you're telling me we can talk anywhere, anytime and not just at the computer. I hear what you are saying, but I am in no mood for your word games, or your sarcasm either. Please don't be mad. I don't mean to be impertinent. I'm just frustrated!!

I am not mad at you for your honesty, child. I am never mad at you for anything.

Thank you Grandmother, for your love and patience with me.

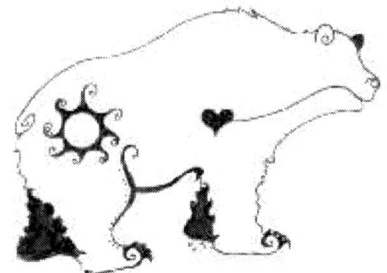

(Later that day)

Conversation Sixteen continued

We talked in the car, did we not?

Yes, Grandmother, we did. Will you please tell me again so that I may write it down?

Certainly, child. You had expressed concern that you would be a liar and lead people astray. You fear that you may make things up just to tell people what they want to hear. Hear me now . . . You do not *know* what they want to hear. But I do. You do not have any desires of your own in regard to other people that I may speak to. You do not know them intimately enough to know what it is they want to hear. You do know that they want to hear truth and to be uplifted and comforted and to be taught. In other words, you desire the best and wish them to reach their highest potential however that manifests in their lives. That is my desire also. So we are in agreement on that. I will express the things they need to hear in order to do that. You be concerned only with allowing me to speak and do not be concerned as much with what I will say when I speak.

Now Grandmother, no disrespect meant here, but there's no telling what You might say and that scares me!

Indeed. It is also what makes it so exciting to converse with me, true? (Smile) Just know that I will never say anything to hurt anyone, and I will never

speak anything but the truth. But remember the talk we had about truth and how it may differ for people. Let me speak and do not try to color the content with only what feels true to you. You have prayed to be a hollow bone and now you have the opportunity to be just that.

Grandmother, I went back and re-read what you told me about the elder I wanted to study with. You did not tell me that I would be her student, only that I would learn from her, which I did. So you were right!

Yes, indeed I was. But continue with your thought, please.

Well, you also told me very specific things about a ring I bought and how it would help to accelerate the energy if I wore it while doing Reiki. That doesn't appear to have come true. So what's up with that? I made that part up, right?

No child, you did not. Let me ask you something now. Did you take the ring and use it the way I said it could be used? Did you practice Reiki with it on your finger while believing that it would accelerate the energy?

No, you know I didn't, Grandmother.

Then how do you know it's not true if you haven't followed instructions?

I guess I don't. But what about the alleged priestess who had the ring before me? Now that really is hard to swallow. You said that she would be one of my guides too and that I could talk to her the way I talk to you.

I did. And have you done so? No, you have not. When you wish to do so and feel comfortable enough to connect with her, you can talk to her the way you

talk to Me. I also tell you again not to be constrained by your concept of time. How the ring could have come to you from such a long time ago is what makes it hard for you to believe. Remember that time is not linear. Perhaps the ring came from another dimension and was manifested in this plane just for you! Free yourself to think outside of the box, child. Entertain concepts that feel entirely foreign to you! Stretch! Grow! Trust! Explore!

Grandmother, that explanation blows my mind! I will try to think outside the box from now on.

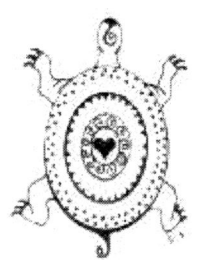

(Next day)

Conversation Seventeen

Grandmother, why would a soul choose to incarnate at this late point in history? I mean 2012 is so close and a child born now will only be a toddler when whatever is going to happen, happens. It seems like maybe no more souls should be coming to this plane and only those already here should be working to bring about change as 2012 gets nearer. What will happen to the babies and young ones that are here for the drastic circumstances that might occur?

The young ones and the babies will have the same choices that all the other souls have. They can stay and help the Shift take place, or they can go to the other plane and not be here, but assist from the other side. Just because a soul is clothed in a young physical body does not mean that it doesn't have the capacity for making decisions on a soul level. Indeed, the children coming to Earth now are different from all the children that have come before ... They come in with the knowledge and do not forget it. They will carry the divine message in their hearts. Unlike past generations who forget who they really are as they age, these children do not forget and will remember the message always. These special children, Indigos and Crystal children and Rainbow babies (known as such due to the colors of their auras), have been coming to Earth for many years and each cluster of souls that comes has gotten stronger and more enlightened. Indeed, the young

ones play a very important part in assisting the Earth with the Shift of energy that is taking place.

Thank you, Grandmother. I have to leave soon to go to my mom's. I wish I didn't have to go today. I would rather stay here and talk to you.

Child, wherever you go, there I Am. We can talk anywhere and anytime. Never forget this, for I will begin to speak more and more often to you, and not wait until you sit in front of your computer. That will be for your inspiration alone. However, when you begin to bring forth my words publicly, it would be good to record them in some manner so that people may remember what was said to and for them. I can hear you already saying you don't want to make tapes and charge money for them! We will find a way to make the messages permanent in some form. Do not worry. And now you must leave for your visit with your mother. It is a good thing that you are doing, bringing peace and joy to your mother in her elder years. Honoring her in this manner is the very essence of what you are called to do. The power of the Divine Feminine is never more obvious than in the relationship between mother and daughter. Now you nurture her and the circle is complete. The healing of your childhood wounds has enabled you to extend healing to your mother. Know that you are helping to prepare her for a smooth transition.

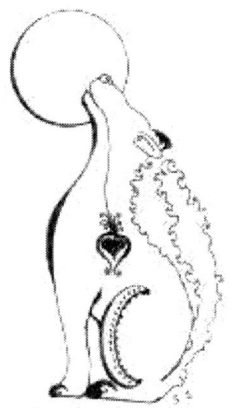

Summer 2008

Conversation Eighteen

Grandmother, I am going to ask the ladies in my Friday morning group to let me practice standing aside and letting you speak. Is that okay with You?

Child, whatever you need to do to feel more comfortable with the process is fine with Me.

There is no set way in which I will speak to people, not at this point.

If people want to ask questions, that is good. Or if I wish to just bring forth a message, I will let you know and you can allow Me to do that. I know you have been thinking about the concept of Me being a conglomeration of energies, or the mass consciousness of creation etc. But you knew this from the beginning. Remember when you asked me who I am and I said to pick one, for I am all of them.

Yes, Grandmother, I do remember. But it feels more personal for me to relate to you as Grandmother so I will continue to call you that if it is alright with you.

Child, you may call me whatever you wish. I know who I Am and I answer when I Am called. Tell me what else has been going through your mind.

Well, to tell you the truth, I feel very protective of my relationship with you. I want for it to be just us. It's okay if someone else hears from God/Goddess, but I wish the

Grandmother part was just mine. The other day I felt jealous when my friend said, Well, Grandmother told me . . . I know that's selfish and I am ashamed to admit it, but it's true. And I know you already know it anyway.

That is one reason I revealed myself to you as Grandmother. If I had said; "This is a conglomeration of cosmic energies and I greet you." You may not have heard me, or believed me. But because I Am not just one single unit or being, many people can talk to Me and communicate with Me. Indeed, everyone can if they choose to. Do not be bothered by what others call Me. They each have their own connection and each connection is different and special. Your connection to Me is unique and not the same as anyone else's. You have read about the Sisterhood of the Shields and it is a representation of the feminine, or Goddess power. So also is the Council of Grandmothers. The Grandmother energy that is coming forth today is a manifestation of the Divine Feminine that is seeking to re-establish herself in the world. She is sorely needed. There must be a blending of energies for the Earth to be healed. Not just masculine and not just feminine energy. There must be a sacred marriage of these two energies. However, the feminine energy will be dominant for a period of time. This is necessary to bring back the balance that was lost when the masculine took over to such a great degree. Just as a pendulum swings back and forth from side to side before finding the center and balancing straight in the middle, so will the energies do. But eventually the middle will be found and balance will be restored again to the Earth.

Thank you, Grandmother. I know that bringing your messages to people is one way that I can personally help to restore the balance that you speak of.

June 13, 2008

Conversation Nineteen

Well child, you have the first individual meeting with someone today who wishes to hear from me. Relax, and let me speak through you. I will bring forth the message that this person needs to hear. Did you hear Me say that I would give the message, not you? Trust that the words you hear in your mind will be My words. They are coming through you, not from you. You stumble on the fact that the words you hear are in your "own" voice. Thus, you think they are your words and not mine. I will give you a signal to let you know that I am ready to speak and that the words coming from that point on will be from me. I will also tell you when I am finished and you will know that the message has ended for that moment. When you are doing individual sessions with people, they may ask questions if you let them. I will decide at that point if I will give a personal message or not. And no, I will not tell them something that feels crazy or scary for you to tell them. I will not, for example, tell someone to quit their job and just trust that money will come to them! I will say none of these things that feel weird to you and probably to them too! That type of message a person has to hear from them selves and not through another channel. I have told people directly to do things like that, but I will not tell anyone through you to do that. Be assured that the messages I give for you to speak are uplifting and loving words of wisdom to help people cope with the world as it is shifting and changing. I may speak to people about their attitudes and beliefs, and I may (nay, I will) speak to people about issues that need to be addressed in order for healing to occur in their lives. This is the primary purpose of the messages . . to bring healing into the lives of the ones who seek you out to hear from Me. This is not entertainment. And it is not for *you* to prosper financially (though you *will* prosper, not only financially, but in other ways as well). Always hold *healing* in your heart as your goal and your reason for letting Me speak. If this is your focus, you need never worry about your motives, or fear that you are leading someone astray through your words. If you truly desire healing for the ones who come and I know that you do, then all the rest will fall into place as you trust and let Me speak to people.

Grandmother, this feels like a very big thing to do, and I am not sure that I am worthy or able to do it.

Child, are you worthy and able to open your mouth and speak? That is all you need to do. That . . . and trust. You are able to trust, for you have shown that over and over again in your life's circumstances. And you are worthy of far more than you ever dreamed of. Go and look up those two words in your dictionary.

Grandmother, *worthy* means having value or merit.

Yes, I know, child. And indeed you have value to me. You are valuable beyond measure. Now look up the word able.

It says having enough power and skill to do something.

Yes, child. And since you have unlimited power, you are able to do this thing to which you have been called. Indeed, have you not fought every step of the way against doing this? How could you ever fear that this is your own doing? If you desired it for fame, fortune or glory would you not be running to do it as quickly as possible so that you could achieve all of those things? But child you have hesitated and doubted yourself. These are not the marks of an egotistical mind set. It is time now for you to put away your feelings of inadequacy. The time left is short, and many people have not yet heard the message. I have spoken to many women and men across the planet, and my message is being brought forth for a world that is rapidly shifting and changing. Your way of giving the message will reach the people that it is intended for. Other people with the same message will reach others. The message is the same, but the channels are diverse so as to reach as many people as possible. You will be validated by hearing the same essential message from many different vessels. When someone tells you that they are the ONLY person who has this message, or this method of healing, or this path to salvation, do not be taken in. No one person will be given a message for All the people. Spirit uses many vessels for the work to be done. Not just one person.

Now before you ask about Jesus, remember that his message was also brought forth many years before his birth by Buddha and by many other prophets as well. His way of spreading the message was different and reached the people it was meant for. But other prophets have been sent to reach those in other cultures. When Jesus said that there is only one way to God, He was saying that essentially there is only one message and that is the message to love. He knew that other teachers and prophets would bring the same message in different forms. Look behind the written words of Jesus and see the intention and truth behind them. It is not sacrilegious to dig deeper and to figure out for yourself what His words meant and what they were saying to you personally.

(Later same day)

Conversation Nineteen Continued . . .

When you place your intention on hearing from Me, then the thoughts that come to you will be from Me. Your intention is what makes it so. I come through the channel of your rational mind and yet I bring knowledge that you could not access except through your connection to Me.

Grandmother, people have started to seek me out in order to hear from you. I am not used to having people seek me out for anything.

On the contrary child, people have always sought you out. Remember in the churches you attended how the ones who were broken and needy would always find their way to your doorstep? This is no different. Now many people will be seeking you and you can help them more today than you could back then. You were not much past being broken yourself in those days, correct? Today you have a wholeness that you hadn't yet achieved then and you will be able to do more for the ones who come to you. I will be there always, speaking, leading and guiding you. You thought then that your bundle was to show people the way to salvation. Today you know that your bundle is to bring the Divine Feminine into form in your own life and in the lives of others.

Grandmother, tell me more about the Diving Feminine and the Goddess. I still have enough left over religion in my head to feel sometimes that I am dishonoring God by acknowledging the Goddess. They still feel separate to me sometimes and so I am not always comfortable with addressing Creator as Goddess. Why is that? I know that they are the same, just different aspects of the same creative energy, but it feels more personal to address God, or Jesus.

Child, how much closer could God be than to be inside of your being? God is so personal that He/She is a part of you, God IS you, remember?

Yes, but this He/She thing is annoying and I am tired of typing it and worrying that I might offend someone by just using one or the other!

Then stop typing it. If it is annoying to you, do not use it. Call the Energy whatever you wish to call it. Remember that God knows his own name and will answer when someone calls it, no matter what name they choose to use when they call.

Regarding the Sacred Feminine let me say this . . . "She" is the pronoun to use when speaking of this aspect of God. Perhaps that is one way you could remedy the He/She thing that is annoying you. *She* is the feminine energy of God and *He* is the masculine energy of God. It is two sides of the very same coin, if you will. It is one God-coin that has two distinct sides, purposes and attributes. They are not separate, only distinctive and different. One without the other is unbalanced. The balance is shifting now. In the past, the male energy, or masculine aspect of God, if you prefer, has been dominant. Dominant, in a very suppressive way to the women of this world. The energies coming through now are

predominantly feminine in nature. This is necessary, as I have said before, in order for the pendulum to swing back into the center. Women have a very important role in the times to come. They must teach the men how to be nurturing and caring in a way that is not threatening to their manhood. Men must realize that to get in touch with their feminine side does not mean to turn into women. It means allowing the part of them selves that is loving and nurturing to have its place in their lives. It does not mean to be soft or to lose their masculine attributes. Men were created in one way and women were created in a different way. Not that the creation process was different, but that basically they are wired differently if that makes it more understandable. This is just how things are. It makes for many interesting and enlightening experiences together, does it not? (Smile)

Sometimes I wonder what God was thinking when he made us so different! It doesn't seem fair that men are so unfeeling and insensitive to the women in their lives.

But not all men are insensitive and unfeeling as you put it. Some men have begun to wake up and allow their feminine energy to become a part of their lives. More and more men will be going through this process as the women become stronger and stronger. The feminine energy continues to pour into your planetary configuration. It is all part of a grand plan, impossible to perceive from one perspective. Do not let the interactions with the men in your lives become a stumbling block in your growth. They have their own timetable. This was all ordered and planned in such a way that the most harmonious merger could take place. The shift that is talked about is largely a result of this merger. If possible, do not take personally the difficulties that may arise in your male/female relationships due to this merge of energies. I am not suggesting that any woman stay in an abusive relationship. I just encourage my daughters to try and have a larger perspective of the events that are occurring on your Earth. Although uncomfortable at times, the lessons that are to be learned and the knowledge that can be gleaned from these interactions with your men are extremely valuable. Each energy has much to teach the other. The feminine energy is more "spiritual" due to the fact that it is a creative energy that can give birth to so many things. Indeed, it can and does give birth to babies, to dreams and ideas, to wisdom and to light. And that is just to name a few! When the two energies become unbalanced in your own life, or in the life of a planet, the result is the same. Masculine energy, when not balanced by the feminine, can be destructive and cause many ills. In a single life it can cause aggressiveness, criticism, anger, and violence. On a larger scale, it results in wars, poverty, prejudice and the like. Feminine energy when not balanced by the masculine may become passive, scared to act and depressive. The perfect balance of these two brings harmony into all your relationships and into all global interactions as well.

Thank you, Grandmother, for that beautiful lesson on energy and balance.

Conversation Twenty

Grandmother, I was wondering about something. Sometimes even now, I still have doubts about the reality of you in my life. Even after all of your lessons. Will that ever go away?

Perhaps so, child and perhaps not. It is entirely up to you. The doubt you feel is doubt of yourself, not doubt that I am real. You know that I am real, but you do not trust your own ability to let Me speak through you. You are concerned with what others will think of you, not what they will think of Me. The ones, who are meant to hear and understand my message, will have no doubts. The message will ring clear and true to those who receive it. To the ones who do not receive it . . . well, that is of no consequence to you. You are the hollow bone for Me to use and what the people do with the message is up to each individual. Your part is only to bring the message. Child, people are hungry today for a message from Spirit. Look around at all the readers and channelers that are appearing all over your planet. Some are speaking from ego, but many are authentic and people are flocking to hear them. That is how great the hunger is today. Even if people don't know exactly what it is that is happening on your planet, they sense that something is. This hunger is what makes the need so great for souls like yours to be open to the process of having Spirit speak through them. The fear that you may lead someone astray is unfounded. If you are pointing them

toward God, then they cannot go astray, for God is the only place where they can end up.

Grandmother, what if someone asks a very personal question for guidance about what to do in their life or in their relationship, or with their money? You know . . . something really important like that. What if I gave them the wrong advice?

Child, people have minds of their own and have the ability to discern, weigh and judge messages for themselves. Also remember that when someone asks a question, they most likely already have an answer and are looking only for validation. Most people have a strong enough ego and will do whatever it is that they want to do, in spite of anything someone else tells them. Gently remind them to follow their own intuition and trust Spirit as they hear it speak in the stillness of their own heart. Child, know this and tell the ones who come to you, not to trust those who say they have the only way to enlightenment. If someone tells you that they have the only way to be healed from past trauma, or the only way to be free of past life karma etc . . . then be cautious. They may indeed, have a good way of doing these things, but there is never only one way to do things. This assertion comes from the ego, the desire to be in the spotlight and perhaps the desire for monetary gain. Indeed, if one could possess knowledge of the only way to do something, then people would pay large sums of money to be healed or enlightened, or whatever the claim is. You need not pay huge sums of money to have your DNA reactivated, or your chakras cleared, or your past lives accessed! There are teachers in these areas, true and they deserve to be paid for their time and expertise, but an extravagant amount of money, along with the claim

of being the only one who can do whatever it is, should be looked at carefully. And if people would only realize it, they are able to do all of these things themselves. You child, can access your own past lives, activate your own DNA (I love that one), research your Akashic records, talk to the angels, the fairies and do anything else you wish to do. However, most people do not know that they can do this, or do not know how to do this. This is where teachers come into the picture. So teachers are valuable. But the true teacher has a deep desire for the student to surpass them. You do not teach in order to make the student dependent upon you. You teach so that they can do things for themselves and then teach others. It's like parenting a child, and as the saying goes, you give them roots and wings. Root them in God, and teach them to fly.

Grandmother, thank you for these beautiful teachings. You always give me so much to think about.

You are welcome, child. Sleep well now.

June 21, Sunday

Conversation Twenty One

Hello Grandmother. Someone asked me recently about the vortexes in the Earth. Could you tell me something about them?

Indeed child, I can and will. Your planet has many energetic centers that may be referred to as vortexes. The word vortex pertains more to the cone shape of these energy centers than anything else. These centers are akin to the chakras in the human body. They are places where energy is swirling in a downward motion, and creating a cone of magnetic, energetic momentum that helps to keep the Earth anchored in her orbital pattern. Just as the human body has many centers that might be called pressure points (as in acupuncture, or acupressure), so does your Earth Mother. Some of these spots that people call vortexes are actually places where thousands of years of ceremony have taken place and the energy has collected into such a magnitude of power that people can actually feel it. Others are centers of energy that have been there since her inception. These vortexes were placed there for a specific purpose. They will be opened, or activated, if you prefer, as the need arises and when the time is ripe. Yes, you humans can help to open these vortexes with your prayers and with your intentions. But they will be opened with or without your help, for that is the plan and that is their purpose. They were put here to assist in the great shift that is so rapidly approaching. But when you do choose to

assist in their opening, it will benefit you greatly and will help to hasten the process. In this way it will benefit you; as they open up, more and more energy will be brought into your atmosphere from the etheric plane and from other dimensions. These energies will be filled with light, information and healing power. Some of these vortexes will even be portals for other beings to contact your race. Indeed, these portals have been open and active for many years, but most of the population has not been ready to accept the presence of Others. Sadly, many humans would be quick to kill or destroy any life form that they are not familiar with. This is due largely to fear. Humankind has such an enormous collective ego, that many of them actually believe that you are the only form of life in this whole vast, constantly expanding universe. How ridiculous! As many different forms of life as there is on your planet alone, these are a mere speck compared to the life that exists outside of your experience. The love of God is so great that it can extend to as many beings as you could ever possibly imagine and even more. Expand your mind! Expand your concept of who and what God is! Now, believe beyond even that limitation.

Grandmother, you are telling me such awesome things and here I am getting frustrated with my computer!

You do fret yourself over the most trivial things, don't you, child?

Yes, but if they are important to me they are important to you too, right? (Grin)

Yes, they are. But in a match of wits, child, you cannot beat me. So rest now and we will play tomorrow. (Smile) Know that I love you.

And I love you too, Grandmother.

July 1, 2008

Conversation Twenty Two

Good morning, Grandmother. I have been in a frantic state of mind and haven't come to speak with you in several days.

I am aware of that, child. Have you decided to let go of all those trivial matters?

Well, I am trying to, Grandmother. But with all due respect, I don't think that all of it is trivial. Some of it feels big to me!

Yes, that is the problem. They FEEL big to you, but that doesn't mean that they ARE big. Do you understand the difference? If you view your problems in the light of eternity, they are indeed very small. You must change your perspective. What will all of these issues matter in a few years? There's that word again . . . *matter*. Do they matter at all? No, not if you don't make them matter. If you do not turn them into physical matter with the power of your imagination and the strength of your intention, then they will not take form as matter in your experience. You have been imagining all kinds of problems in your mind with the constant chatter of *what if this* and *what if that*. This must stop in order for you to have peace. Instead, form images in your mind (use your imagination) of peaceful situations and stress free circumstances. Thank God for all that you have and do not worry about whatever you think that you don't have. For I tell you, child, there is nothing that you do not have. All that exists or ever will exist is at your fingertips. Remember how I told you that we . . . that is you and I . . . exist in different

dimensions, or on different levels of reality? Although there is really no you or I as we are ONE, but for the purpose of this lesson let us use those words. As above, so below (on Earth as it is in heaven). This means quite literally that the way things are where I am, is the way things can be where you are. It is within your power to bring this to pass. I am here, where all things already exist, and are just waiting for you to bring them into the physical form of matter where you are. Step one is imagination, step two is intention, and step three is manifestation. If you can imagine it child, it is possible. Do not let the term imagination cause you to stumble. Your imagination is one of the most precious gifts that Creator has given you. Imagination is the brush you use to place the paint of your intention onto the canvas of your life in this physical plane. Remember that analogy . . . paint, brush, canvas. Imagination, intention, manifestation. It really is quite simple, you know. You are the one who is painting the picture of your desires and dreams and hopes onto the canvas of your life. Pick up the brush (imagination), put some paint on it (intention) and create a masterpiece (Your life!).

Wow, Grandmother! I like that example!

Thank you child, I have a million of them. (Smile)

You can be so funny sometimes, Grandmother. I love how you kid around with me.

Indeed child. We do have fun together, do we not? Is there something else you wish to discuss before you have to leave for your day?

Yes, there is. Last night someone called and asked about becoming my apprentice. It is feeling sort of overwhelming to have people asking this kind of thing and treating me as if I am something special. Why are they doing that? I am the same person I always was.

You are stepping into your own power and people recognize that and truly wish to learn from you. Plus, you have much to teach. However, some people are dazzled by your title of Medicine Woman and want to attach themselves to you in order to get something that they perceive you have. This may be power, knowledge, or any number of other things. These people will sap your energy and try to steal your power from you. Most do not do this intentionally, or even consciously. You have to recognize what each person wants from you, and what you are willing and able to give and how you are being guided by Spirit for each student that appears in your life. This will come more naturally to you as you continue to walk the path of a Medicine Woman. Do not flinch when you hear that title. It is an honor and a privilege and you know what you are. You have studied diligently, and worked hard to gain this title, so now you must wear it and bring the respect to it that it deserves. Do not bear it lightly, child, but do not get so bogged down by the title that you lose sight of what your work is. In the final analysis, it truly does not matter by what title you are called. It only matters who and what you are. Now, you must leave for your visit with your mom and I will be with you all the way. My love for you knows no bounds, child.

And neither does mine for you, Grandmother. Thank you for your beautiful lessons.

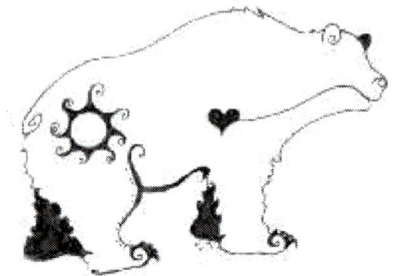

July 3, 2008

Conversation Twenty Three

Good morning, Grandmother. We hired a dog sitter for our trip to New York, and I am upset over the way she has finagled another $25 out of us! It makes me want to do something mean to her in return. I hate it when I have feelings like that. How do I stop reacting that way when I think someone has wronged me?

Well, good morning, child. Let us again look at the words you have chosen to use. Before you used the words "I feel as though" . . . and we explored that. Now you have used the words "I think that" . . . Let us look at that, shall we?

Okay, Grandmother. But I THINK I know where this is going!

That is humorous, child. And you are right. Thinking is what gets you in trouble. Your thoughts make things to be as they are. If, indeed, you think this person has harmed you, then it is so. If, instead, you do <u>not</u> think they have harmed you, then they have not and <u>cannot</u> harm you. As you think it, so it is. Now, why not try thinking that this person is performing a good service for you by taking care of your beloved pets and that they deserve to be paid for doing that? Whatever problems they may have in their thinking about money does not need to affect you. Perhaps they have not yet learned to trust the universe to provide all that they need and are

instead looking to customers to provide for them? **Then you can be a blessing to this person by giving the extra $25 that you are so concerned about. What a wonderful opportunity for you and your husband to bless someone else and in turn to learn to trust more fully in your own lives that all your needs will be met. Consider that this person may have a need that requires $25 to fulfill it and has prayed for God to send the amount they need. Now consider that you and your husband are the answer to their prayers. I have asked you to be the conduit for their blessing! Embrace this lesson and learn it fully so that you can move on to more important lessons. Not that this one isn't important, but there are others that will carry more weight in your life than the matters of money and finances.**

Grandmother, thank you for this wisdom. It makes such good sense to me and I do believe it, so why is it so difficult to stay in that place instead of returning again and again to the place of being angry about it?

As I have said, child, it is your thoughts that keep returning to it. Guard the thoughts that try to come into your mind. When you hear them approaching and you know they are not thoughts that you want to have, tell them that they are not welcome and that you will no longer entertain them.

Grandmother, I went ahead and looked up the word entertain in the dictionary because I knew you were going to tell me to! It says to keep up and maintain; to hold the interest of; and give pleasure to. But the one that really got me was the one that said to have as a guest! It also said to allow oneself to think about. But Grandmother, if I have a negative thought as a guest in my head, that is really bad!!!

It is neither good nor bad child, but it certainly does not serve your highest good, nor does it help to fulfill your purpose here. If you allow the thoughts to enter your mind and then take up residence as a guest, you have created an atmosphere where they can grow and thrive and even multiply. Instead, invite positive thoughts into your mind as guests. Tell them that they are welcome and invite them to multiply and grow and flourish. Soon, your mind will be filled with loving, positive energy, which is what all thoughts are anyway. They are energy.

July 18, 2008 Friday

Conversation Twenty Four

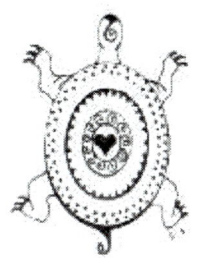

Hello Grandmother. I have missed being with you like this. On the computer, I mean. So much as happened during the past week and a half! Our trip to New York was very nice, even though a bit hectic and stressful. And then to come home and be in a car accident that damaged the car and gave me whiplash was not what we had planned!

Indeed, child, it must feel very disjointed and hard for you to understand. And yet, things are moving along according to plan. You need to believe this and to trust that all is as it should be. It is fine for you to make plans and mostly this is a wise thing to do. However, do not let the plans that you make leave no room for circumstances to change and shift and become other plans that you did not consciously make. You know and understand on some level that everything that occurs in your life is drawn to you for a sacred purpose. Sometimes you will know the sacred purpose, but as often as not, you will not know it. This does not matter so much as does the fact that you believe this and trust that it is so. Be assured that if the purpose is one that you need to know while you are in this dimension then it will be revealed to you at the proper time. If it is not necessary for the growth of your soul at this present moment, then you may have to wait to know the purpose. Let me say this about purpose . . . _everything_ has a purpose or a reason for being, yes, but not everything happens for some huge cosmic

purpose. Some things occur only because of the circumstances that exist in that moment in this dimension of being. Of course, every occurrence has the capacity to be a learning experience, as you humans are so fond of calling them. This does not mean the event occurred in order for you to learn something. In other words, that was not the purpose of the event. But inherent in every event is the chance to learn something about your self. Do not say to yourself, *"Oh, God made me ill, or let me become ill, so that I could learn such and such."* God does not make you ill, or let you become ill in order to learn. In like manner, God does not cause car accidents to happen, or disease to occur so that you can learn a lesson. When these things do happen due to circumstances that exist in this dimension, then by all means, look for a way to learn something about your self and about God. But do not *ever* think that God *made* them happen to you.

Thank you, Grandmother. Once again, you have given me much to consider and think about.

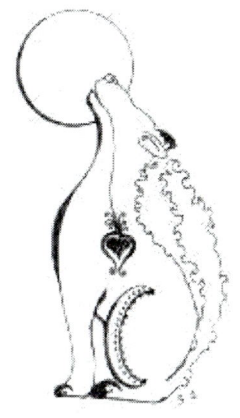

July 23, 2008 Wednesday

Conversation Twenty Five

God morning, Grandmother.

Good morning, child. Look at what you just wrote. You typed *God morning*. I know you think it was just a typo, but I say to you that this is indeed a God morning, as is every moment of your life. Every moment is a God Moment. Every event is a God Event. Every circumstance, or situation, is a God Circumstance or a God Situation. In other words, God is in everything and God IS everything. Thank you for that *typo*, child. It was a wonderful opportunity to tell you, once again, something that you are all inclined to forget sometimes. Now tell me, what do you wish to talk about today?

Well, some women are coming over here today to hear you speak. Is it cheating to ask you ahead of time what you wish to say to them? Does this make your words any less pure or true?

My words through you are pure and true always. But remember that they are filtered through your own spirit and indeed are a product of your higher self (which is God, because God is everything), so they will have the flavor of you own individual personality. You like things to be simple and easy to understand, not too complex or complicated and not a lot of cosmic gobbledygook (your words). So then, this is the manner in which I will speak through you. I speak differently through different people. Keep in mind however, that I do reserve the right to say

things through you that you may not understand at the time. When this occurs, I will make it plain to you at a later time what I intended by my words. And I know the word "intend" has been much in your mind this morning, due to the discussion you had with a friend about intentions. So go and look it up in the dictionary, child.

Grandmother, the word *intend* means to have as a plan or an aim to do something.

Indeed it does. And you thought, along with many other people, that it was a magic word, didn't you? It simply means that when you intend to do something, or set your intention, that you make a plan to do that thing. Then you must put forth the required effort to accomplish that goal, or to reach what you aim for. You cannot say, for instance, *I intend to be a better person today* and then continue to act in ways that do not serve that purpose. You must consciously choose to act in ways that fulfill that intention.

Now child, it is getting close to time for you to leave and you are still wondering about your initial question. The answer is no, it is not cheating to ask me beforehand what I wish to speak to the group about. Do not try to get a message and memorize it, for there has to be spontaneity and fluidity to what you are bringing forth from me. But for you to have a general idea of what I wish to address at each group, or even private sessions, is okay for now. If it helps you to feel more confident, then by all means we can do that. But there will come a day when this is not necessary for you. You will reach the place where you can spontaneously bring forth my message by simply stepping aside and letting Me be there.

Now let us address what I wish to speak to the group about today, shall we? I wish to speak today about Love. Love is not just something you do. Love is a living, breathing entity. Love is the Creator. You have heard it said that *God is Love* and this is indeed the truth. Love is the glue that holds the universe together and it is the building block for all of creation. It is the reason you have all incarnated onto this planet . . . to learn how to love and be loved. To learn how to love each other, love yourselves and Love God. This is the subject I wish to speak about today to those who are gathering at your house.

Thank you, Grandmother. I will be open and I will stand aside so that you can speak your message of love.

(The small group of women did gather at my house and in spite of my fears, Grandmother spoke to them about love. Her message was well received and this made me very happy.)

My friend Jane, had been leading drumming circles for several years, but hadn't done any in awhile. After I shared with her that Grandmother had spoken publicly at my Friday morning group the day I was supposed to teach on the Medicine Wheel, she invited me to join her at the drumming circle and allow Grandmother to come and speak there.

July 25, 2008 Friday

Conversation Twenty Six

Good morning, Grandmother. Tomorrow night is the first drumming circle and I had a weird dream last night. I dreamed that I was in a school play and could not remember my lines. I was terrified of being in front of an audience and kept saying "I can't do it, I can't do it!" Finally, in my dream, I dropped out of the play and felt devastated by my inability to perform. It doesn't take a genius to figure out what that's all about, does it?

Indeed not, child. Your fears are threatening to overcome you and you must not allow that to happen. We have many things to accomplish together and many people to reach with a message of hope and love. Now I will talk to you a bit about the message I have for those who will come to the drumming circle tomorrow night. I wish to speak about walking with one foot in each world. The physical world is where the flesh body lives and the spirit world is where the real person dwells. One must be grounded in this reality and also have their spirit in touch with the other reality. At times, this may seem difficult to do. You have all come here to this dimension for a specific purpose, but you belong in the other realm from whence you all came. You are here to learn lessons, to experience different situations and to learn how to love one another, yourselves, and God. While in this Earth walk, you are subject to certain laws, certain rules and certain conditions. Most of these do not apply to the spirit world that you left to come here. So for some, it can be a difficult transition to make. But be assured that Creator knows all about you and each individual

Earth walk. Creator has a specific plan for each life. Do not fret yourself by saying, *Oh dear, what is my purpose here?* Your purpose is programmed into your very soul and you will always be shown what to do and when to do it. The purpose of your life may not be, indeed, probably will not be, to change the world on a grand scale. The purpose of each life here is to touch with love every other being that crosses your path. Every other being, in every kingdom of beings, that exists. The animal, plant, and mineral kingdoms as well as the humans you come in contact with. There is also a vast realm of other worldly beings that many of you have not encountered before. Be assured that they are also part of the Divine Plan and they will be showing themselves very soon as the day approaches when the veil is lifted. These being are inter-dimensional and can now accomplish many things that humans have not yet aspired to. In the days to come, they will be teachers for the human race. You on Earth, have a tremendous role in the vast drama that is being played out in the universe at this time in history. This planet was created specifically for the purpose of being a testing ground, a learning place for spirits to come and take on flesh for the purpose of experiencing many emotions.

But let me return to the subject of having one foot in each world. How do I do this? you may ask. Indeed it is quite simple really. Just acknowledge that while you are clothed in flesh you are subject to conditions that arise here. But remember that no condition is unchangeable, because of who you really are. Keep your feet grounded on Mother Earth and keep your spirit reaching for the stars. And in this way, you will walk between two worlds. Give what is due to each dimension. The Bible says, "Render unto Caesar what is Caesar's" and indeed this is good advice. Do not be afraid to prosper financially, for that is the method of exchange in Caesar's world at this time. This will change and it will change sooner than might suit some people, but do not forget to render unto the spirit world what is due also. By this, I mean to feed your spirit, acknowledge your gifts, USE your gifts and do not fear them. Every person has a special gift, something that they can do that no one else can do in just the same way. It is meant to be this way. Diversity is a wonderful gift from Creator and indeed, makes your life on Earth interesting, does it not? Feed your spirit. Walk your path, whatever that may be. Pray, meditate, chant, dance, drum, sing and celebrate your journey here. It is not meant to be a hardship, but a tool for evolving your soul to a higher plane of existence. The mass consciousness is being raised to a different vibration. Just as a radio can be tuned to different stations to pick up new messages, so can your consciousness be tuned to a higher frequency to receive messages from the spirit realm.

As I stated previously, certain laws apply here on your Earth that do not apply in the realm of pure spirit. However, the laws that apply in the spirit realm DO apply here also. For instance, "as above, so below" applies here as well as in my dimension. "Whatever you sow is what you reap" also applies here. You need look no further than your garden to see this truth expressed. Do you plan pumpkin seeds and expect a watermelon to grow? Of course not. By the same token, you cannot sow the seeds of hatred, bitterness, and unforgiveness and expect to get back love. You must sow the seeds of love in order for love to grow. You can plant a seed every day simply by smiling at a stranger, encouraging a friend, or talking to your animals.

Are there any other laws that apply to both realms, Grandmother?

Indeed. One of them is the law of attraction. You will attract to yourself and into your life, that which you think about most. If you think about your problems constantly, then more problems will be attracted into your sphere of experience. Often the things you perceive as problems are opportunities for you to change, to evolve, and to tune yourself to the higher frequency that we spoke of earlier. The secret is to know that every circumstance that comes into your experience is one that you planned ahead of time. You do not consciously remember doing this, so when something occurs that feels unpleasant, you perceive that you have a problem. However, some things do come into your life that are merely the result of conditions that exist in this plane and these are often viewed as problems also. Use these things as opportunities.

If you think that something is a problem, then it becomes one and the more you think of it, the faster it is attracted to you. As you think it, so it is. When a situation arises that may be a challenge for you, view it as an opportunity instead of a problem. It will be whatever you view it as.

Oh, but then you say, I will attract challenges into my life and they are really problems that I am supposed to view as challenges! Do not play mind games with yourself. Know that everything that comes into your life is MEANT to be there and can be seen as an

opportunity, or as a problem. The things that I am speaking of are intangible. You will attract love, peace, joy, hope, prosperity and forgiveness into your life if you think of these things. You can and will attract these things into your life if you trust and know that whatever befalls you, it is all in the Divine Plan and can be used to further your spiritual growth. The Plan that you and God drew up together, before you incarnated and put on your flesh suit, was designed with much love, forethought and for very specific purposes. Your eternal soul knew exactly what it wished to accomplish on this trip and so you made a Plan especially suited for that purpose. Each joy and each sorrow is designed to bring you closer and closer to Creator. Each accomplishment and each failure is meant to be a stepping stone to higher planes of consciousness. Every childhood issue, each trauma, was put into your life so that you could see how far above those hurts you could rise! They are meant to help you see how Divine you truly are. They are sent to help you understand how forgiveness works and how unforgiveness can hold you back from attaining the spiritual goals you have set for yourself.

Thank you, Grandmother. As always, you have given me so much to think about!

Conversation Twenty Seven

Grandmother, I hear a lot of talk about the old ways. Can you tell me something about that?

It is time to return to the old ways, the ways of the Ancestors. It is time to treat Mother Earth with the respect that she deserves. You must recognize that she is a living, breathing entity and not just an inanimate object that you can use and misuse for your own gain. When you take one of the gifts that she offers so freely such as herbs, or flowers, or plants, or food, please honor her by not taking more than you need for the moment. And always give her something in return, whether it is tobacco, cornmeal, or even your own saliva as the old ones used to do. In this way, you are saying Thank you, Mother, for what you have given us, we honor you. This is a goodly thing and a pleasing thing to do. Live your life in a proper way and give respect to all creatures that inhabit the Earth with you.

So, honoring the Earth is an important part of following the old ways. What else, Grandmother?

Do not place yourself above or below any other. Some have a higher consciousness than others and it would surprise you all to know which ones these are! But all beings have a spirit and are part of Creator. Indeed, did Creator not say when he looked upon his own creation, "It is good?" Then who are you to say that some things are not good? All that was created is good and serves a purpose. There is a grand

scheme at work in the universe and you . . . all of you, are an integral part of it. Do not ever think that your life is unimportant, for it is a significant piece of the puzzle that is being put together. It is a beautiful thread in the tapestry that we are all weaving together. It is one silver note in the symphony of music that all of creation is singing. Together we are creating the future and I tell you that it is a bright one. There are times of change and challenge that lay before you, but you are more than equal to the task. Mankind stands on the brink of an exciting and shining new day in its history. All over your planet, people are awakening to the fact that they are divine beings who can accomplish more than they ever dreamed possible. As more and more light floods your planet, more and more people will awaken. It is indeed an exciting time to be alive.

Thank you, Grandmother, for all of this information. And you're right, even though it might feel scary and uncertain at times, it really is exciting.

You are welcome, child. As you know, I have been whispering to you about walking in harmony with all your relations. I wish to speak to you about that now if you are willing to listen?

Of course I will listen Grandmother! Tell me how to walk in harmony.

Well first of all, harmony is not two notes that sound exactly the same being played together. Harmony occurs when two different notes blend together to make a pleasing sound. There might be a low note and a high note. These two notes are vibrating at a different frequency in order to make their individual sounds, but when played together they blend into a harmony. Harmony exists when two or more notes that are different are put together and used to form a sound that is fuller and richer than the one note would have been alone. So it is in relationships also. When two or more people are joined together, even though they may be on different frequencies, they can sing a beautiful, harmonious song. The song will be fuller and richer than one they might have sung alone. There is a time to sing alone, and a time to sing in chorus. Now is the time to join the chorus and create a harmonious whole that can begin to heal your planet! I am speaking of spiritual matters here. It is time to put aside your differences and concentrate on common beliefs and compose a song of harmony to sing your planet back into alignment with the universe.

Grandmother, that is a beautiful analogy. How exactly do we all learn to sing in harmony?

Your mass consciousness is one of lack, scarcity, pain, sorrow, greed, war and poverty. It is time to join together and sing a song of wholeness, completeness, healing, joy, tranquility and love. It is time for all of you to be channels of the Light that is breaking upon your universal consciousness. Many of you are aware of this Light and live in its brightness. But some of you have not yet opened your eyes to see this Light that is pouring into your consciousness. Each time you have a healing thought toward someone else, or send up a prayer for healing, or refuse to judge, you are helping the Light to burn brighter. We are all assisting the planet and helping her to be reborn into a new state of being. She is returning to her original state of well being. I tell you that Mother Earth was created into a state of total health and wholeness. It is the actions of humans that have caused her to be in the state that she is in today. I am not judging or scolding humanity now. I am simply telling you how things are so that you can assist with bringing them back to where they were meant to be.

In the beginning, Mother Earth had all that you, as a race of humans, needed to survive. She produced all the plants, and herbs for healing and food that were necessary for your survival. As you became denser and denser in your form and vibrated at a slower rate and became stuck in matter, you gradually lost the ability to see things as they really are. You began to think in terms of lack, greed and such. This has continued until the present age, but is going to change in a very short amount of time. That is "time" as you know it. As Mother Earth has been used and misused for so many years, she is depleted now of her original resources. The fear of not having enough has caused many to gather more than they need. As more and more people and nations did this, the Earth began to run out of supplies. Now indeed, you are in a state of lack. This is what greed and fear have caused to happen. I tell you that when people begin to live from a place of abundance and plenty, the situation will change. As more and more people change their vibration to one harmony and move away from the notion of mine and yours and indeed come from a place of ours, Earth can and will replenish herself. She is in the process of cleansing. The natural disasters and *Acts of God* that appear to be so harmful are nothing more than a way for her to rid herself of old negative energies. I am not saying that the ones who transition during these occurrences are negative, do not misunderstand. But do understand that death is not a tragedy.

Change your perspective on death and your feelings about these things will not be so frightening. Realize that these people chose to make their transitions during a time of disaster and they are souls who are evolved enough to be willing to do this as the cleansing of the Earth takes place. This intention was scripted into their life plans before they came here.

That is pretty deep, Grandmother. I guess these were very brave souls.

Yes, child. And every soul that chooses to come to Earth, especially the ones who chose to be here at this time, are brave souls.

August 6, 2008

Conversation Twenty Eight

I was sitting with my mom in the nursing home when Grandmother began to speak to me. I grabbed my ever present pen and notebook and started scribbling down her words. I love it when she just starts a conversation out of the blue when I haven't even really asked a question, or consciously tuned in to her. It helps me to see that she is always with me and always ready to speak. But then as I listened to her, I realized that she was answering a question I had asked, or that I had been thinking about. I had been mulling over some of the things she says about God and the question I had, is what she was answering now.

Child, do you not yet know that God is ALL there is? It is not just that God is in all things, the truth lies in knowing that God IS all things. You are God. I am God speaking to you. The Earth, flowers, trees, stars and planets, the very air you breathe is God. God is made manifest in millions of different shapes, colors, and forms. God is matter and takes on visible aspects so that you might know God in many different ways. The idea that God is one big body, usually male in gender, that sits upon a throne somewhere out there, is a child's fairy tale. The reality of God is so much bigger than that. Does your Bible not say; "When I became a man, I put away childish things?" Now indeed it is time to put away your childish concepts of God. "*Childish*", meaning too small. However, being child-like in your faith is a different matter. A child is curious and free, eager to learn and experience. A child is filled with belief and

wonder when he hears of magical things. Indeed, I implore you to have the heart of a child . . . one that loves without fear, expresses emotions honestly and is always open to whatever life has to offer. A child knows that there is no cause to worry about where the next meal is coming from, or how they will pay the bills. A child trusts his father and mother to provide all that is needed. You also can trust your mother/father God to care for you in all ways and for always.

I am aware of the fact that many of you did not have human parents who did these things for you and therefore it is difficult to accept or trust the concept of a loving parent. But I ask you to trust your emotions at this very moment. Do you not feel a longing for that which I speak of? Do you not feel at some deep level that what I tell you is true? Trust that knowing inside of you. Know that there is indeed a Mother and Father who are not human and therefore not subject to being anything less than perfect in the way that they take care of you and love you. Now take that knowing a step further and accept that this loving energy is what you call God. It is LOVE personified and it is, indeed, all there IS. It is all things and it is *you*. *You* are this LOVE. *You* are this JOY. *You* are this PEACE.

Grandmother, this all sounds wonderful. But how do we experience ourselves as these things on a practical level in this dimension?

When occurrences in your Earth walk cause you to feel less than joyful, know that there is a supreme purpose in experiencing them. Here is a paradox: Pain, hurt, and sorrow are tools that can be used to make room for more joy in your life. As they hollow

out spaces in your soul, joy rushes in to fill them. It has been said that nature abhors a vacuum. So know that if there is a vacuum or empty space, in your spirit, left by some past event that was traumatic, <u>know</u> beyond a doubt that if you allow joy access to that space, it will indeed rush in to fill it.

Thank you, Grandmother. I am going to bed now, and I will talk to you again soon!

Good night, child.

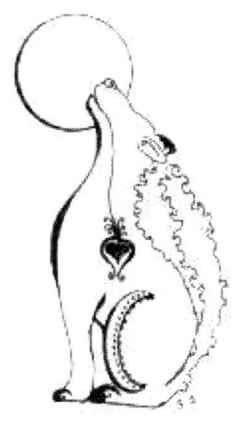

August 19, 2008

Conversation Twenty Nine

Hello, Grandmother. What do you have to teach me about today?

Good morning, child. Here is today's lesson. Do not hesitate when you have received your vision. Do not let fear cripple you, or keep you from trying new things. Expand your comfort level. Do things that feel unfamiliar to you. Let uncertainty fall by the wayside as you explore all the options that are available to you. There are so many ways for you to be healed, so many paths that your feet can walk upon and you are limited only by the smallness of your own vision. In the days to come, life will change in ways that some people will find difficult to cope with. But the ancient ways will be re-established and your world will be better for it. As you have already begun to see and experience in your own personal life, this is a period of cleansing and clearing out old patterns, old relationships and old beliefs that no longer serve your highest good. As you grieve the loss of these things, know that they will be replaced by something new, or perhaps re-fashioned into a new form. Nothing real is ever lost, so do not fear the readjustments that are taking place with your friends, your loved ones, your careers and your finances. This seeming upheaval in the personal lives of people mirrors the events occurring in the world around you. As I have told you before, Light and Love will be the building blocks for the new constructs that are, even now, being put into place. Fear and greed will no longer

be the base for any structure to rest upon. Do not expect that these events will occur instantaneously, but understand that they are in process and have been for many of your Earth years.

Once again, child, I remind you not to be taken in by those who claim to have the only way to do something, or become something. Universal knowledge is limitless and is available and accessible to any and all who wish to avail themselves of it. Indeed, there are as many different ways to do something as there are souls to access the knowledge. Variety . . . diversity . . . these are the hallmarks of creativity. And Divine Source is continuously creating. Creating, re-forming, changing and expanding, endlessly and for eternity. I understand that this concept is difficult for you to grasp through minds that have been trained to deal with a linear and finite time line. But when you transcend the boundaries that exist only in your mind, what wondrous truth and light is waiting for you!

September 2008

Conversation Thirty

Grandmother, I am having many different emotions about a relationship in my life that is really changing.

Good for you, child. Emotions are nice to have, are they not? (Smile)

Yes, well, these emotions are baffling. I don't know exactly what is going on here. With my friend, I mean. Why is this relationship dying? I know you told me that our relationships would be changing along with a lot of other things. But I guess I didn't realize how difficult and painful it would be to let go of some of them.

As I have often told you, child, nothing ever dies. It simply changes form. Remember we spoke about the ebb and flow of life? Well, you are experiencing the ebb at this point. You will continue to notice things changing in your life. Old relationships and old ways of being, are falling away to make way for a new form to take shape. Your life is being refashioned into something brand new and trust me child, you will like it. Have you noticed how much easier it is for you now to remain silent when that is necessary and how much easier it is for you to speak when you need to?

Grandmother, tell me about the word power. It holds sort of a negative charge for me. What's that old saying that absolute power, corrupts absolutely? What about that?

Do you have your dictionary handy, child? (Smile)

Well of course I do, because I have learned by now that you will ask me to look up every word that I have a question about! Okay Grandmother, I looked it up. Although it does say things about authority and force and stuff, the first definition was very revealing to me. It simply says; *the ability to do, act, or produce.*

Indeed. And do you not have these abilities? You have the ability to DO whatever you wish, the ability to ACT in whatever way you choose and the ability to PRODUCE anything that you desire. This is the meaning of personal power. You have the power to do, act, and produce in your own personal life the things, people and circumstances that are needed for you to achieve the highest good for the plan that you have laid out.

So power is not about controlling other people?

Not in the truest sense of the word. Your language sometimes causes difficultly in explaining certain concepts, due to the limited meanings ascribed to the words. Of course, some do take the word "power" and use it to mean that they can control others. But this cannot be done without the consent of the one being controlled. It may be an unconscious consent, but nevertheless it is a consent that is necessary in order for the one *in power* to be able to control them.

But what about people who are forced into slavery, for instance. Surely they didn't consent to that! What about the laws and rules of society that we have to follow or go to jail? Don't those control our behavior?

Ah, but are these people really being controlled? Or are they just following the rules to the best of their ability in order to live? Do they have a choice of

whether or not to do this? Of course they do. Therefore they are not being controlled so much as they are just making necessary choices. Do you see the difference?

I suppose so, Grandmother. But if someone says, "Do this or die." it still feels very controlling to me.

That's because you still tend to think of death as an ending. As you know, death is only a change of form, a change of location. It is nothing to fear. If one has no fear of death, then there is nothing another can do to control them. The attitude becomes one of; *go ahead and do what you will. Death will only release me back to the form I once knew; therefore I do not fear it.* If death is the worst threat that this world can make, then there is, indeed, nothing to ever fear.

Thank you, Grandmother. That is very comforting and really true. I mean if the worst thing that can happen to you is death and that's not bad, then you really don't' need to be afraid of anything. I think I finally truly get that!

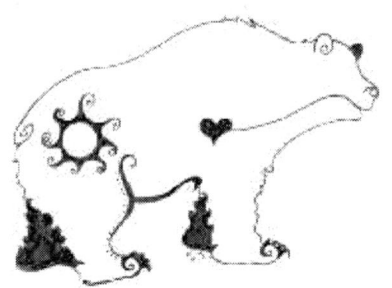

October 2008

Conversation Thirty One

Grandmother, the presidential election is on my mind these days. Can you tell me who to vote for? (You know I am just kidding!)

Indeed, I will tell you who to vote for. As you look inside of your own spirit for guidance, know that whoever you vote for is the one I want you to vote for. Also know that I will do this for everyone and that each will hear from me a different message.

Then you don't have a favorite candidate, Grandmother? (Smile)

Indeed, they are all my favorites. Even the ones you do not particularly like. I love all beings equally, as you are well aware. Child, in these troubled times people are grasping and searching for the human leader that will rescue them from all that is happening around them. I tell you that there is no leader on your Earth who can do that. Study the issues, if you wish. Make an informed choice, as you are able. Then exercise your right to vote as your heart leads you. But do not think that whoever gets into office, as they say, has a great deal of sway over what is happening on your planet. The events taking place now and events that are still pending, are ones that have been forming for many, many years. No one person is responsible for that. The person in your White House will be the person whose life plan included that occurrence as part of their purpose.

So are you saying that things are predestined and that we have no effect on anything here? If that's true, then why bother to vote at all? In fact, why bother to do anything? Why not just sit back and let the chips fall where they may?

No, I am not saying that at all. It is not predestination in the sense that you mean. Rather, it is a softer meaning, often phrased as; "things are just as they are supposed to be". There is a difference, do you see? Your part in the drama is to make wise choices, follow your heart and trust that all things work in the manner that they were meant to. If everyone does that, then Divine Order takes precedence over individual desires.

Wait a minute. This is getting worse as we go along. Now you're saying that individual desires are not important? That group mentality takes precedence? Isn't that how things like the Holocaust occurred?

Child, you are not listening. I said that Divine Order takes precedence, not group mentality. And Divine Order always has the needs of the individual at heart. Divine Order always works for the highest and best good of all beings, not just one. Remember that we are all connected in this Web, so what affects one, affects ALL. Think not so much group as family.

Once again, Grandmother, you give me so much to think about and to process. Thank you.

November 2008

Conversation Thirty Two

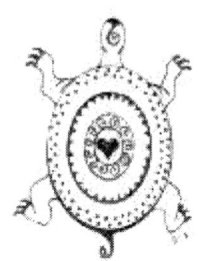

Good morning, Grandmother. I lost a few of the pages that I had typed out and stored in the computer and they had some of our conversations on them. I get so upset with myself when something like that happens.

Yes child, I know. You get yourself upset over many inconsequential things, do you not?

I guess so, Grandmother. But I am getting better, right?

Indeed, child. You are growing by leaps and bounds as they say.

Grandmother, some of the things happening seem to be happening so quickly! People are asking me to come to groups and let you speak. People want personal messages from you. You even have a mailing list now to send out weekly messages.

I know, isn't it wonderful? I find it amusing child, that you have been working and praying for many of your Earth years for things like this to happen. And now that they are, it seems quick to you! Do you see more clearly how your time frame in this dimension works?

I know that there really is no time as we think of it here on Earth, that it's just an illusion. It is a construct that humans invented in order to exist on some sort of schedule. Right? But I'm not sure I completely understand how it works.

the same as ten thousand years in the vastness of the never ending essence of eternity. Is that any easier?

Maybe a little. Let me see if I've got the idea. Ok, so my soul knows that there really is no time, even as it realizes that I have to move within that framework in this physical world. But if I move into my spirit while I am waiting for an answer to my prayers, then time disappears and it really is unimportant when something happens? So then, to my soul, ten thousand years would seem like a mere second.

Indeed. And instead of trying to move into your spirit, just be who you really are. You are an infinite, never-dying, always changing, piece of God. (Creator) who has taken form as the human person called Laughing Heart. I do, indeed, understand how difficult it sometimes is to grasp these truths while still in the flesh suit of your Earth walk. The reality of existing outside the perimeters of limited time will soon become more and more apparent to humans. Indeed, some of you have already felt the impact of how time is speeding up, so to speak. Continue to play with time, as you have been doing and see how much you can change your human reality.

You mean like when I made time slow down so that I wouldn't be late for my group last week? That really was cool Grandmother! I only had ten minutes to get there and I live about twenty minutes away. So I just made my intention be that I would not be late and I think maybe I said a little prayer too. Then time just sort of "crunched up" and I got to group and had several minutes to spare! Remember?

Exactly. By the clock, you had not enough minutes to get where you were going without being late. (Being late is another illusion, by the way). You were able to

suspend your belief in what the clock told you and by your intention and your willingness to experience something beyond your everyday reality, you indeed, arrived on time. For that space in eternity, you existed outside the limitations of time. And I am telling you that it is possible to do that <u>all the time.</u> (Smile)

Grandmother, my mind feels like a rubber band that has been stretched too far and is ready to snap!

Then by all means, child, it is time for you to stop and rest.

Very funny, Grandmother. I love that you joke with me and make me laugh, while making me think of things in ways I never have before!

And I love the way you make Me laugh and how you let your mind expand and try so hard to understand, even when My lessons seem to make no sense to you.

Thank you, Grandmother. I think I will go to bed now. I look forward to talking with You again.

Sleep well, child.

And I did.

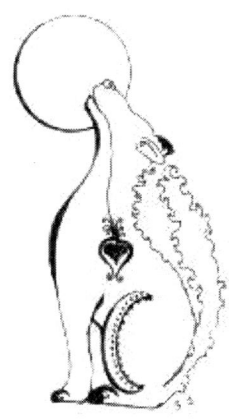

September 2008

Conversation Thirty Three

Good morning, Grandmother. Today is the Psychic Fair and You are going to be doing readings there. I feel a little tense, but I'm not sure why.

Good morning, child. You are feeling tense because you are focused on how much money you might make and on how frightening it feels to you to let me speak to people on a personal basis. Focus instead, on how wonderful today will be as you let Me spread My message and as you share your talent for creating art with the people who come to the festival. See the difference? It is just a subtle shift of your focus. Usually, that is all it takes to change the way you might be feeling . . . just a small shift in your focus. It also works in the opposite direction. You may be feeling very positive about something and a tiny thought enters your mind that is not so positive. Immediately the human mind tends to flow toward that thought. The focus has shifted, do you see? And your mood becomes one with the negative thought vibration. Before you know it, you are in a bad mood. That is why it is important for you to be aware of your thoughts and of the thought process that your mind goes through in the course of a day. Over a long period of time, these vibrations build up and you will draw to yourself the vibration of your thoughts, whatever they may be. It does not happen overnight and one small negative thought will not pull disaster to you! This idea is what keeps you in doubt about the

validity of this particular concept. You do not want to judge yourself every time you have a negative thought, or feel that you have caused bad things to happen by an occasional thought. I understand this, and you are correct. ONE thought will not do this. Or even an occasional thought will not do this. But, as I have said, over a period of time (and now the time is getting shorter), these thoughts will build up a certain energy and they carry power. You *can* draw to yourself the particular vibration that your thoughts carry over a period of time. This is not a strange new age idea. Did not Jesus, the Master (and many other Masters) say that "as a man thinketh in his heart, so he is?" That is exactly what that statement means. You become whatever you think about. How do you become something? By drawing to yourself the circumstances and situations that result in forming the way you react to others and to your own self. Your thoughts are what draw these circumstances and situations to you. Therefore, what you think is what you become. This is an important concept for you and for everyone to grasp. Hold this teaching in your heart child and make it a firm belief in your life.

I will, Grandmother. You have told me time and again that my thoughts are what get me in trouble too often! Thank you for this teaching. I will do my best to do as You ask. And thank you for being so patient with me!

It is My honor and My pleasure to teach you child. Indeed, teaching these concepts is My purpose for manifesting Myself to you and speaking to others through you.

After this conversation with Grandmother, she began asking me to let her speak publicly more often. Because of this, I did not write down our interchanges as frequently as I had done before. We also started sending out a weekly message via e-mail. However, I am feeling very drawn to keeping a written account of our continuing conversations again. She has assured me, with a wink and a grin that this is probably not the last book she intends to write!

As I allow myself to trust and to become increasingly more aligned with her energy, she opens doors for me to walk through . . . doors that present opportunities for me to bring her message to an ever growing audience. Yes, I am still fearful at times, but as I step out in faith and allow Grandmother the liberty to use me as her channel, the freer I become.

I am including in this book the weekly e-mail messages that she has brought up to this point. Each one is a complete lesson in and of it self and so is presented with no introduction other than to name the topic of discussion. They are in no particular chronological order even though She does at times address certain holidays and global occurrences, which are self explanatory.

Thank you for the privilege of sharing Her messages with you. I hope that something has touched your heart and helped you in some way.

Grandmother, I love you and honor you with all of my being.

Aho.

Messages from Grandmother

Summer 2009

Message on Illusion & Reality

I come bringing greetings and love for each of you today. I
am, as you know, the energy that Laughing Heart calls
Grandmother. I present myself in this manner as I have
found the Grandmother image to be comforting and familiar
to most of you. If, however, this image is not comfortable for
you, then feel free to picture me however you choose. My
form is not important, although the Grandmother energies,
or the Feminine Principle of Creator, are flooding your planet
in these days and that is indeed, what I am. I am just one
color in the Rainbow of Love that Creator is . . . one facet of
the prism, so to speak.

I wish to speak to you, briefly, about a subject that would take
many of your hours to fully cover. That subject is your
concept of reality and illusion. Sometimes it is difficult for
you to tell the difference between the two.

Your reality is whatever you believe it to be. For example, if
you look at the state of your economy and believe that it is
bad, then for you, it is. When you hear about scarcity and lack
and accept and believe what you hear as truth, then it
becomes your truth. These then, are the things that
manifest in your life. You will experience scarcity and lack as
your reality. However, you can choose to see a different
reality. You can choose to see the illusion of the material
world and believe that Creator can and will, provide
everything you need in spite of what the world is telling you.
By doing this, you will experience, as your reality, abundance
and provision in all things.

Do you see? **Your** reality will be experienced by you as
whatever you believe it to be. Someone else may be
experiencing a totally different reality in their life, but each
individual's experience of reality is whatever they perceive it

to be. You can be living in the exact same circumstances in the world and yet be experiencing a completely different reality. The illusion is that what you can see and feel and hear and taste, are the things that are real. In truth, it is exactly the opposite of that. The unseen things, the abundance that is yet to be manifested, is what is *real*. The things that exist just beyond your physical senses are the *reality*. All else is an illusion. You have put this illusion in place yourselves, by your beliefs and for the purpose of learning how to experience Truth in the face of illusion.

How very brilliant you all are! I stand in awe of your magnificence.

With love,

I AM,

Grandmother

New Energies Coming In

Greetings Children. It is I, the energy that Laughing Heart
calls Grandmother. I have need to speak to you once again.
The energies that were brought forth during the Summer
Solstice were those of a cleansing and purifying nature. You
have found yourselves facing personal challenges like never
before. Old belief systems, old habits of behavior and old
thought patterns are being reconstructed. You are
experiencing a variety of physical symptoms. There are vague
and unexplained aches and pains in your bodies . . . sinus
drainage, flu-like symptoms and such. These are a clearing
out of old issues. Things that you thought were over and done
with have surfaced again. Old memories, hurts and
disappointments are being brought to your mind; often at
night just before you enter the dream state. This is for the
purpose of releasing them once and for all. Do not be
troubled by this. Just know that you are being emptied of old
stuff in order to make room for more joy and love than you
ever thought possible. Two things cannot occupy the same
space at the same time. Let go of the old so that the new can
come in and take over.

Your relationships are being tested and tried. Many of you
are feeling the need for solitude, while others are being
pulled toward community. This is not a contradiction. It is
simply that people's needs are different at this time. You have
probably noticed a change in your eating habits and many
foods that you used to enjoy no longer appeal to you. This is
due to the physical changes in your bodies. You are being
prepared for a new way of eating . . . a more natural way. Pre-
packaged foods will not be available at some point in the
Shift. The nutritional needs of your bodies are changing.

Spend as much time as possible outdoors in the sunlight. Be
vigilant in your self care. Get enough rest, although many of
you do not need as much sleep as you used to. Again, this is

due to the changes occurring in your bodies. On the other hand, some of you may need more sleep than usual. Give your body whatever it is telling you it needs. You must learn to listen to your bodies, for the medical system will go the way of all the other establishments that are being torn down and rebuilt on a new foundation.

You can heal yourself. This may not happen overnight, but ultimately you will be your own doctors and healers. Trust your instincts and become familiar with how your body speaks to you. How you feel physically is the best indicator of what is going on for you emotionally and spiritually. Many factors are involved, true, but generally speaking when your body is feeling discomfort; it is a good time to take a closer look at your emotional and spiritual state.

Love yourself. Do not judge yourself. Do the best that you can and know that this is always enough. You are greatly valued and loved by Creator. This is a wonderful time to be alive. Do not be taken in by the fear that some are trying to instill in you with tales of the failing economy, natural disasters, famine, flood and such. This process of humanity's evolution is happening right on the Divine schedule and all is as it should be.

Be At Peace,

Grandmother

As the Cleansing Continues

The energies coming through at this time are highly intensified. Your senses are greatly heightened, and all that you feel and perceive is magnified. As you continue to be emptied out and purged of all that is *old* and no longer necessary or useful, you will find that your psychic abilities are being honed to a much sharper degree. The issues that are surfacing and presenting themselves for the purpose of healing and release will be felt at a very intense level. Now is not the time, generally speaking, for you to confront other people with your issues and to try and get *closure* by dealing with other people, or discussing old hurts that you feel are unresolved etc. It is instead, a time for going inward. It is a time to seek peace and acceptance inside of your self. It is about being honest with yourselves and discovering what things you are still holding onto that may interfere with you becoming the vessel of light that you are meant to be.

As the cleansing continues, be aware of the inner voice that speaks from your heart. Information that is channeled for you through someone else can be useful and informative, but you really have no need for a teacher other than your own spirit, in tune with Source. As long as there are people who do not trust their own inner truths and are hesitant about trusting what they know to be true, there will be a place for channeling, intuitive readings and so forth. But know that eventually, each person will be the source of their own information. As you grow in awareness and sensitivity, you will find the ability to hear the voice of Spirit becoming stronger and stronger. Do not be afraid to hear and trust this voice. As long as what you receive does not instruct you to harm yourself or any other being, it is good information.

Imagine a future where every individual is completely connected to Source; Each one receiving direction and instruction directly from Creator. All living and working in harmony and peace, as Earth is restored to her original purity and beauty and humankind reaches its full potential. All races, colors and creeds living together as one family. Where war and discord, hunger and poverty no longer exist. This is not a dream children, this is indeed, the future that is being realized and that is being brought forth into form. Face your future with an open heart and with joyful anticipation, for it will be worth every bit of the difficulty that you are experiencing now in order to manifest that future.

You are loved,

Grandmother

The New Paradigm

When the new paradigm is firmly in place and the New Day has fully dawned, there will be no room for things such as bitterness, anger, unforgiveness, hatred, judgment, or criticism. These things cannot and will not, exist in this new world of peace and plenty, love and light. As these emotions come up for you more and more in these present days, know that you are being emptied out and cleansed from them. They must be brought into the Light and exposed so that you can let go of them. When old memories of hurt, disappointment or sorrow are brought to mind, feel them if need be, but do not cling to them. Let go of them as soon as you are able to. It is not that you have a lot more work do to. It is simply that you have something else to release. That is a choice on your part. If you keep that old issue in your mind, going over and over it again and again, it gains strength and power. Remember that what you focus on is what you manifest. So do not linger over these issues. You are being prepared to hold the light energies of the new paradigm and everything about the old has to be brought into the light in order for it to be transmuted into what will be acceptable in the new energy pattern. When you see the escalation of violence and hatred, know that it is being forced to the surface by the light for the purpose of being exposed and done away with. It cannot remain hidden, so it is surfacing for all to see and so that all can rejoice as it is brought down and destroyed. These things are occurring on a personal level in each individual life and also on a global scale.

Do not fear the changes that are taking place in the world and in your own lives. Everything is being shaken and what is left standing will be those things good and true and real. You cannot lose something that is real. If you lose it, then it was not real to begin with. Do you understand this? Even through death, you cannot lose someone. Death is merely a change in form and a move into another dimension. **Just because**

you can't see something does not mean it isn't there.
Remember this in the days to follow.

All IS WELL,

Grandmother

Message on Energy

Greetings and love to each of you. I am the energy that Laughing Heart calls Grandmother.

I wish to speak to you today on a subject of great interest. It is the subject of Energy. As you know, all things are Energy. You are Energy and I am Energy. Every living thing and everything that you think of as inanimate is made of Energy. All energetic beings are vibrating at a certain frequency and this includes you, in your physical bodies. Some beings vibrate at a higher rate than others and are therefore lighter, as opposed to being heavier, or denser, if you prefer. This is neither good nor bad. It is simply the way things are. You will be **attracted** to beings that are vibrating at the same energetic rate that you are vibrating. By the same token, you will **attract** to yourself those beings that are vibrating at your same frequency rate. Your vibration is subject to change in direct response to the emotions that you are feeling.

Sometimes it takes only a single thought to change your vibration, to lower it, if you will. You have heard the phrase; *that person or situation really brings me down*? This is exactly true. Protect yourself from any person, place, or thing that causes your vibration to drop in frequency. It is a proper thing for you to do, but resist the temptation to judge what you are protecting yourself from. Do you understand? Practice intentionally carrying your vibration at a higher rate and see how much lighter you feel. You can do this in any number of ways. Being very aware of your thoughts and keeping them as positive as possible is one way. The food that you take into your body also affects the rate at which it vibrates. I have no preference as to whether or not you eat meat, although there has been much discussion among you regarding this subject. Let Me just say that as you learn to listen to your body, it will tell you what it wants to eat and not eat. As a general rule, vegetables and herbs vibrate at a higher rate than does the meat you eat. This is mostly due to the killing process that the animals are subjected to. There is no respect, no honoring of the animal's sacrifice and the fear they feel is absorbed and stored in their bodies, which in turn you eat. Clearly then, you are absorbing their vibration of fear. But if you must have meat, then make your prayers of gratitude to them before you eat. Again, there is no need to get bogged down in rules and regulations about how and what you eat. As always, your intention is the most important aspect of how you do anything.

With great love,

I AM,

Grandmother

The Old Ways

Greeting to you all.

It is with much love that I come to speak to you about a return to the old ways. Returning to the old ways does not mean for you to sell your homes, live in tents and hunt for game with bows and arrows or cook over an open fire! (Although if you desire to do these things, it is good and proper. It is also guaranteed to bring you closer to Mother Earth and closer to truly appreciating how much you depend on her for your very existence).

Returning to the old ways is more of an attitude shift, a shift in your energy, if you will . . . a change in your pattern of thought. Your energy must shift from the attitude of *getting*, into the attitude or energy of *receiving*. You are not *getting* something from the Earth Mother, she is graciously giving to you and you are *receiving*. Receive with an open and grateful heart. THIS is the old way. Never take more than you need for the moment. Always remember to give back when you receive. Walk with gentle steps upon Her bosom and leave each place where you spend time better than it was when you got there. Respect all forms of life. Know that each being is a part of Creator and is filled and fueled by its own individual spirit. Demonstrate this knowing by the way you treat and interact with creation. There was a time long ago, when all of mankind walked in this knowing . . . a time when peace and harmony were experienced by all. There must be a return to this way of being in the world.

Learn again to listen. Do you remember the song of the trees? Learn to hear it again. Learn to hear the songs of all beings, for every being has one that is its own unique sound and message. They will sing for you if you will tune your ears to listen. Listen and love.

Being tuned in, respecting all life, receiving gratefully and walking gently is the old way. **It is time to remember.**

Aho! I AM,

Grandmother

Message on Extremes

Greeting to each of you, I am the energy that Laughing Heart calls Grandmother.

I want to address once again, the issue of **extremes** that some of you are hearing in these days of great changing and shifting. Be wary; no, not worry . . . rather, to look closely at any extreme. Balance is present in all things. Balance is a universal principle and one that is necessary. It can be tempting to say that since your life is scripted before you come into the physical, all you need to do is sit idly by and let the plan unfold as it will.

It is true that your Earth walk is ordered and that you had much input into how things would occur. The lessons you desired to learn remain the same, but the manner in which you choose to learn them is not written in stone so to speak. The extreme at one end of the spectrum says your path is pre-destined and cannot be changed. This can lead to a victim mentality. *It* happens to you and you are at the mercy of the fates.

The other extreme says nothing has to happen unless you want it to. This can lead to judgment, superiority and condescension. When a challenge presents itself, it is thought to be a result of negative thoughts or not having enough faith or some other failing on your part. The Truth . . . as always, lies somewhere in the middle of these two teachings.

Your thoughts, belief systems and attitudes greatly affect how you respond to events in your life. An event that may seem disastrous to some can be experienced with peace and serenity by others, simply because of the way they choose to view it. So while some occurrences are meant to be, the outcome and the effect of these occurrences is up to you. Do not become a victim of your life, but do not become the bearer of complete responsibility. Know that you are **co-**

creating with God, but God holds the ultimate power. Creator always has your best interest and your highest good in mind. So realize that this is a **partnership**, then relax and enjoy the process of experiencing life knowing that while you steer your own vessel, Creator stands at the helm guiding every step of the way.

With love, and in balance,

I AM,

Grandmother

Message on The Shift

Greetings and love to each of you. I am the energy that Laughing Heart calls Grandmother.

There are two extreme theories about the Earth's ascension process that are being sent out today. These theories are causing some fear, some confusion and some misunderstanding. I wish to give my input for your consideration, if that is agreeable.

The first of these theories says that you must be fearful of the coming events. You are encouraged to grow your own food, store away water, move to the highest mountain to avoid flooding and other disasters. Some even go so far as to advise you to stockpile weapons to guard the supplies you have hoarded away. This scenario is indeed *fear* producing. "Be prepared for the worst" seems to be the motto. At the other extreme is the theory that says with a poof of fairy dust and a burst of magical light, you and the Earth will be transformed instantaneously. This event will occur at the moment when enough people have achieved enlightenment and the collective consciousness of mankind reaches a critical mass, thus providing the necessary condition for this to occur. This scenario is much more palatable to most people, as indeed it would understandably be. However, the truth lies somewhere in the middle of these two extremes. As in all things, a balance exists. It is, in all matters, a good practice to be prepared. It is also very good indeed to expect the best and hold positive thoughts for, as you know, your thoughts will eventually take on physical form and become your reality. So, what does this mean for future events and how you will experience them? First, there will be no instantaneous shift into a higher vibration. Indeed, has this change not been going on for many years now? It is a process, not an event. When every soul that chooses to become awakened has done so, the shift will be complete. This could appear to be happening in the blink of an eye, but in truth has been a long time building to this crescendo. Second, there may indeed be challenging times ahead. All around you the entire social structure that you have known is falling apart. It must be so. New systems are waiting to be put into place. But by holding the vibration of love and light in your heart and by trusting Creator to provide for you and care for you, your discomfort will be minimal. The affirmative thought to hold is this: "Creator loves me greatly and will provide all my needs." Love, trust and faith are the keys to finding the balance between these two extremes and experiencing the shift in a positive way.

I AM,

Grandmother

Grandmother's Christmas Message

Greetings and much love to each of you. I am the energy that Laughing Heart calls Grandmother.

As your Christmas time approaches, it is important to remember the reason for the celebration underneath all the trappings. It is a celebration of Love, a celebration of Light and a celebration of the end of spiritual darkness.

It matters little what belief system you hold. It may be the story of the Christ Child born in a manger. Perhaps it is a belief in the coming of the Christ Consciousness as awareness dawns for mankind. It can be any number of different stories, for every culture has its own. But I tell you clearly that the only thing that does matter is the truth that the darkness is indeed, about to be fully lifted from the eyes of humankind.

The Light of complete consciousness and total awareness is being beamed into the hearts and spirits of those who are willing and ready to receive it. The great evolutionary leap, the ascension, the shift, that which has been foretold in all cultures and called by many different names, is taking place NOW. It is cause for great celebration, indeed.

May your hearts be filled with hope and joy, as you reach inside to connect with whatever school of faith that you adhere to. It matters not which faith you have, only that you have faith. Place your faith in the goodness and love of Creator.

With Love, I AM,

Grandmother

New Year's Message for 2009

Greeting to each of you and much love I bring. I am, as you know, the energy that Laughing Heart calls Grandmother.

I wish to speak to you today about the New Year that lies ahead. It will, indeed be a momentous year for humankind. For those of you who may have had any doubts about the radical changes that are occurring on your planet, be prepared to see greater evidence than ever before that your evolutionary leap is all but finished.

Time is accelerating and you will find that your thoughts ideas and dreams can and will, be manifested very easily and quickly. You have noticed that happening already, but the speed at which you can manifest will multiply at least a hundredfold during this coming year. You will amaze yourselves with the things you can do. Be aware that you can manifest in either direction, so to speak. That is to say, the thoughts that are less than useful to you can also be manifested very quickly. So be aware, (not afraid, just aware) of what you are focused on. When you place your attention on the problem instead of the solution, the problem is what intensifies because it is receiving all of your energy. Let your attentions be more solution focused and this year will astound you with the changes that you can manifest in your lives.

As world issues are discussed in your media and their fears are sent out through the airwaves, FOCUS on loving solutions that you personally can assist in achieving. The most effective aid you can bring to your planet is the vibration of LOVE. Hold this vibration to the best of your ability at all times and collectively, all of you will lift the vibrational frequency of the entire planet. When each individual soul holds their own vibration firmly in a place of Love, that energy is strengthened and sent out to others. Love reaches out to love.

And so each individual soul is connected ever more certainly to every other individual soul. This is the deepest meaning of You Are All One . . . connected by the web of love that each soul spins individually and sends out into the universe for others to respond to and to remember their connection with. Wishing you all a year of positive manifestation.

I AM,

Grandmother

The Nature of Reality

I wish to speak to you about the nature of the reality in this plane of physicality where you now exist.

There are certain natural laws that are in effect and that will not be commanded by your thinking. I know that you have been told that you are God and in the most basic sense this is a truth. However, if each one of you was the totality of the oneness of God, there would be no need for each other. Indeed, just one of you would be enough, true? But each individual soul is a spark of God, a piece of Creator existing in the form of you. Together, you make up the wholeness of God. You are able to co-create with God, but there has to be a mutual agreement about what you are creating in certain instances. For example, suppose that you are planning an outdoor event and the weather calls for rain. You pray very hard and affirm as positively as you can that it will NOT rain. You have a positive attitude and you make all of your plans on the assumption that it will not rain because you said it wouldn't! Now on the other side of town suppose that someone is praying very hard that it WILL rain because their garden is dying, or whatever the case may be. Just as you did, they believe and think positively and affirm as strongly as possible that it WILL rain because they said it would! Who wins? Is it the person with the greatest faith? Not so, children. I tell you that the outcome is up to Mother Earth. The decision is in the hands of Nature herself.

This is what I mean when I say that there are natural laws that apply to the physical reality that you are now living in. You cannot control every event in your life. I realize that this is not a popular teaching today, but it is a truth. Now what you DO have complete control over is the manner in which you respond to whatever happens. If it rained when you didn't want it to, or vice versa, you can choose to react in a way that makes you miserable and unhappy. You decide.

Trying so hard to control every little thing is making life a struggle for many of you. Life does not have to be such a struggle. The good times and the bad times are all an integral part of what you came here to experience. Ebb and flow, wax and wane, in and out, expand and contract. It is all part of the process. Just do the best that you can. Love as much as you can. Find beauty everywhere that you can. Laugh as often as you can. Dance, sing, play, cry, grieve, fall down and get back up. Experience your life. That's the reason you are here.

I love you,

Grandmother

Message on the National Crisis

Greetings and love to each of you. I am the energy that
Laughing Heart calls Grandmother.

Today I wish to address the crisis that humanity finds it self
in nationally and indeed, globally.

The first thing you need to know is that ALL IS AS IT
SHOULD BE. Indeed, the events that are taking place on
Earth have been foretold by all of the prophecies of the
indigenous peoples of the world.

This plan for the enlightenment of the Earth and her
inhabitants was put into place eons ago. It is a Divine plan
and you are all aware of it on a subconscious level, a soul
level, if you will. As I have told you before, the old paradigms
must crumble and be done away with before the new systems
can be put into place. This is what you are witness to even
now. It is an exciting time to be here and you all chose to be
here because you have a part to play in the drama that is
unfolding in your planet's history. Do not fear the changes
that are occurring. Know that even though the times to come
may be difficult from a worldly standpoint, you will always be
taken care of. You have all that you need inside of you to live
a life of joy and peace even in the midst of drastic change.

Stay connected to Spirit and trust that everything is moving
along according to Divine Plan. Turn away from the fear that
is sent out on the airwaves, do not believe all that you are
told, do not let greed guide your decisions, and above all trust
your own heart's knowledge and the truth that Spirit
whispers in your ears at night.

This is a blessed time to live on your planet and indeed, a
time to learn many new lessons in faith and hope. Resist the
urge to judge and criticize your leaders. Instead, hold them in
the light and send vibrations of love and truth to them

whenever that urge comes to you. This helps to raise the vibration of love that is being birthed and each one of you is needed in order for the complete change to take place.

All is well. Stand strong and do not fear.

With love,

I AM,

Grandmother

The Great Illusion

Greetings and love to each of you. I am the energy that Laughing Heart calls Grandmother.

I wish to speak to you about The Great Illusion. You all know what it is, but often we need a reminder to help us keep our focus on what the illusion is *not*. Do you find this to be true?

The illusion is that this world and this dimension are all that exists and all that is REAL. *This is all there is* . . . that is The Great Illusion. If you keep your focus on what the illusion is NOT, which is all things of the Spirit and the spirit world, then The Great Illusion holds no power over you. Indeed, the illusion is something that you all played a part in creating. Its purpose is to provide a stage upon which your Earth walk can be played out according to the prearranged plan. But you must always be aware that it is an illusion, something you created to be used to further your soul's growth and evolution. It is not something of any permanent substance, although it seems so at times. Realize that this illusion is as insubstantial as mist and you can walk through it, into the real world of Spirit at will. It is temporary and it serves a purpose, but it is not the real world in any sense of the word. When you are weighed down by the burdens of this plane of existence, remember that you created this illusion for your own growth, look for the lesson in your situation and know that there is a grander plan being played out than what can be seen with the physical eyes.

With Love,

I AM,

Grandmother

Thanksgiving Message 2008

I greet each one of you with love and joy. I am the energy that Laughing Heart calls Grandmother.

In this season that you have set aside in your society to be a time of thanksgiving, I join you in gratitude. I am thankful for each soul, for each open heart and for your willingness to receive from Spirit. I am thankful for the great changes that are taking place and for the level of awareness and enlightenment that exists on your planet. I am thankful for the selfless service that each of you offers to assist in this process of enlightenment.

I invite you to carry this spirit of gratitude; that you celebrate now, into every day of your life. Take the love and closeness you feel for friends and family and extend it to all who cross your path. Do not forget those who are not yet experiencing the abundance that they possess. Be generous with your resources and with your love. Have a continuous attitude of thankfulness and you will be surprised by joy at unexpected moments. Thankfulness opens the door to joy. Being grateful for all that you do have keeps your heart open to receive even more. When you are in the state of gratitude, you are focusing on the positive aspects of your life. This draws more of the same into your experience. Finding even the smallest reason to be thankful is a step toward moving into a place of "receiving".

With gratefulness,

I AM,

Grandmother

Dealing with Chaos

Greetings and love to each one of you. It is with great love and joy that I speak to you this morning. I am the energy that Laughing Heart calls Grandmother.

Flexibility is the key to having peace in the midst of personal chaos. As long as you remain flexible, you will not break beneath the winds of change and confusion that can often blow into your physical circumstances. Remember that your physical circumstances and situations are temporary. Here is a great truth . . . **Nothing is permanent except change.**

When you find yourself in the midst of chaotic conditions, remember to "go with the flow", as they say in your world. This is good advice because nothing that is moving, or flowing, can become stagnant. Bend with the winds of chaos, for if you stiffen and become tense, you stand more of a chance of breaking beneath them.

You do not have to be happy with the chaos, for happiness comes and goes anyway. But if you can manage to remain joyful, which is different from happiness, the chaos will not touch you inside. Remind yourself often that your circumstances are temporary. Have a sense of humor if at all possible. Above all, remain flexible and accept change as inevitable. Nothing lasts forever except my love for you.

With love,

I AM,

Grandmother

Living Close to the Earth

I greet you with joy and with love. As always, I am honored to
come and speak with you. I am the energy that Laughing
Heart calls Grandmother. Today, I have a question for *you*.

What did all the tribes of indigenous people have in
common? What single factor tied them together? What
caused them all to arrive at the same truth even though they
were scattered all around the globe? It is this one fact . . .
They all lived close to the Earth, in tune with Her rhythms
and dependent on Her for their sustenance. Mother Earth
was their provider, their sustainer, their healer and their
teacher. They lived upon her and knew that the seasons turn
in cycles. They understood instinctively that their own lives
did the same. They watched the seeds fall into the ground to
die and then celebrated the new crop in the next fall season.
By observing the new life every year, they understood the
concept of rebirth and resurrection. They watched the
animals mate and were comfortable with their own sexuality
and with the process of procreation. They could see how the
animals cared for their young ones and they valued their own
children. When the old ones changed form, they were put
into the bosom of Mother Earth and there their physical
bodies fed the growth of the trees and plants. When elders
say that the Earth contains their ancestors, this is a very
literal statement. Their feet walked upon the bones of their
ancestors and the ground was sacred where they trod. They
saw that the trees were happy and content to be trees and
they were happy and content with who they were. They
understood that each being has importance and that no one
is greater than, or smaller than any other. They heard the
plants and herbs talk and knew which ones had healing gifts
and which ones were willing to give up their spirits to be
food. They respected all life and walked a path of balance and
harmony. They comprehended that whatever they did to
another they, in essence, were doing to themselves. Without

science or technology, they understood the secrets of creation and knew that the whole universe teemed with life forms, not just those that are visible to the naked eye. They realized that the brotherhood and sisterhood of humankind extended far beyond this world. They knew the meaning of the words; *We are all One*. They lived their lives and walked within this Great Truth. Do not look upon the old ways as foolish or superstitious, but understand that the ancients had tremendous knowledge of life and of spiritual concepts. If you have been searching for a teacher and it seems that one has not appeared, I invite you to look around with an open heart and know that the Earth Mother is the only teacher you need. Everything you need to know can be learned from observing the natural laws that Creator has set in place.

With love,

I AM,

Grandmother

Cultivate Thankfulness

Cultivate an attitude of thankfulness. Gratitude is an energy that vibrates at the highest frequency. It opens the door to joy, love and peace. It brings harmony and balance into your Earth walk by aligning you with the utmost emotion of well being. It is difficult to be depressed or angry when you are thankful.

Gratitude holds your energy in a space where miracles can happen. Gratitude allows you to see things from a different perspective, to get a grasp of the bigger picture. It anchors you into the "now", takes your **focus** off of the future and out of the past. When the past *is* on your mind, find something that you are thankful for in your past experience. And when you look at the future, be thankful for all of the blessings that will be, indeed already are, there waiting for you to experience them. Begin to look around in each moment and find something to be grateful for. Are you grateful that you can see these words and read them? Then thank Creator for your eyesight. Did you wake up this morning able to hear, taste and smell? Then thank Creator for your senses. If you can walk and talk, be grateful for your physical body. If you can't, then be thankful that your mind still works. You see? It isn't hard at all to find something to be thankful for. You just need to make the effort.

When circumstances appear to be negative and hurtful, look beyond the outer reality and dig deeper, until you find even the tiniest thing to be grateful for. Express the gratitude (out loud if possible) and then walk through the open door to peace, love and joy.

In love and gratefulness,

I AM,

Grandmother

Message on Time

Greetings and love to each of you. I am the energy that Laughing Heart calls Grandmother. Today I wish to speak to you about the energetic construct that on your planet is called "Time."

I understand that time is necessary for you to carry out your everyday lives as you go to your jobs, pay your bills, keep appointments and so forth. But in matters of the spirit, know that time does not exist. In the spirit world nothing is ever late or too early. In the realm of the infinite you are in the ever present, eternal, Here and Now. Indeed, eternity may be thought of as "timelessness." So do not fret or be concerned when events do not occur on the time schedule that you are used to living in. Trust that all things are happening just as they were meant to and that they are always right on "time"! (Smile)

Your life, and the life of all on this planet (and others), is working on a divinely planned agenda. The prayers that you have prayed are already **answered** and will manifest in this plane (in the space that you call time) when and where they are meant for your best and highest good.

Be at peace.

With love, I AM,

Grandmother

Spring Message

I invite you to engage your mind in thoughts of rebirth and resurrection during this spring season, for every thought that you have, causes a reaction in your body. Your thoughts release chemicals in your brain that affect your mental and physical health, which raise or lower your vibration. Look around at Mother Earth as she emerges from her long winter of sleep and join her in the celebration of new life. Align yourself with the energy of new beginnings.

Collectively, you stand in the east on the medicine wheel with the golden eagle as spirit keeper. You are emerging from the void and awakening from the winter of slumber. The dreams and visions that you have had during the season past are now ripe and ready to blossom. Your focus has been turned inward as you moved through the winter and now is the time to turn outward and manifest the inner desires that you have gotten in touch with. Just as the new plants and trees, grasses, flowers and herbs are bursting with the life force, so are you!

The winter of introspection has taken you into the void where all things exist, but are not yet visible in your physical reality. Now is the time for you to bring these things into form on this plane. The East is the direction of spontaneity and playfulness. It is the direction for mental healing, the healing of your thoughts. Occupy your mind with thoughts of love, light and peace. Make big plans! This is the season for manifesting your dreams into reality. Just as you must prepare your garden plot by plowing and fertilizing before you plant your seeds, so must you prepare space in your life (and in yourself) before planting the seeds that will grow into the full blown reality of the dreams that you had during your hibernation period. This preparation needs to include gratitude, hope, joy, prayer, deep breathing and mediation, along with planning, action and hard work. Work hard, play hard, but make time to rest. Take good care of yourself and walk in balance. Look around you at the beauty of nature and accept and enjoy every moment as the gift that it is. Remember that unless a seed falls to the ground and dies, a new plant or tree cannot grow. So be grateful to whatever died last season, for it served the purpose of nourishing the new thing that will grow in its place.

Wishing you happy planting,

I AM,

Grandmother

Message on Diversity

Greetings and love to each of you. I am the energy that Laughing Heart calls Grandmother.

I wish to address a subject that has taken on a greater importance in these changing times. Do not be taken in by those who claim to have the "only way" to do something or become something. Universal knowledge is limitless, and is available to any and all who wish to avail themselves of it. Indeed, there are as many ways to do something as there are souls to access the knowledge! Variety, and diversity . . . these are the hallmarks of creativity. And Divine Source is continuously creating. Creating, reforming, changing and expanding . . . endlessly and eternally. This concept is difficult to grasp with a mind that has been trained to deal only in linear time that is finite. But I invite you to transcend the boundaries that exist only in your mind. Do not limit yourself by the smallness of your vision. Know that there are many ways and many paths. The wonderful mystery is that they all lead to the same Source, for there is only One Creator. Remember again, the wheel that has many spokes leading out from the center hub and also back to the center. That Center is Creator. All spokes, or paths, lead to Creator. Indeed, I tell you again, there is no place else to go for Creator is All. Whatever path you choose, it will lead you ultimately back to the Center from whence you came.

I AM, creatively,

Grandmother

Bringing Things Into Matter

I bring you greetings and love. I am the energy that Laughing Heart calls Grandmother.

Hear this truth . . . All things already exist in the spiritual realm, in the Void of non-matter. They are just waiting for you to bring them into physical form and to make them "matter." Step one is using your imagination, step two is using your intention, and step three is manifestation. If you can imagine it, it is possible. Do not let the term "imagination" cause you to stumble. Your imagination is one of the most precious gifts that Creator has given you. Imagination is the brush you use to place the paint of your intention onto the canvas of your life. It really is quite simple, you know. YOU are the one who is painting the picture of your desires, hopes and dreams onto this canvas. Pick up your brush (your imagination). Put some paint on it (your intention). Now create a masterpiece of your life!

With love,

From,

Grandmother

Believe Your Own Heart

Greetings to each of you once again, I am the energy that Laughing Heart calls Grandmother.

Those of you who grew up in the formal church have been exposed to a teaching that is particularly damaging to the spirit and if believed, can inhibit the transformation taking place now in all of you at different rates. It is the teaching that says; *your heart is deceitful and not to be trusted.* It further says that only the written words of any one certain religion or denomination (all man made, by the way), can be trusted as the absolute truth. I ask you all very strongly to understand that this is not correct. Indeed, in these times the heart is the only thing that **can** be trusted. The heart is your gauge for knowing how greatly you are shifting and how you are being transformed into a new way of being. As your heart opens more and more to receive the light and information that is coming to your planet, you will be ever more aware of the changes that are happening inside of you. Yes, some of the changes are physical, and you are indeed being "re-wired" in a manner of speaking. But the biggest change will be the subtle, inner change that takes place in each individual heart chakra. And the broken heart will be *especially* able to assimilate the light and send it forth to others. While the heart is contained, it is not as pliable, not as soft. Once broken, the cracks leave places for the inner light to shine through. Know that the brokenness of your heart is a holy wound that is being used to assist the world in its ascension. You have noticed already how you are responding in more loving ways to situations and people around you. There is no need for defending or explaining yourselves to others. No point in arguing, or trying to persuade others to believe as you do. The heart is the doorway to transformation. Open this door. Love is the glue that holds all things together. Indeed, Love is the very building block of the cosmos. It is not something you do, it is what you ARE.

Sending love from my heart to yours,
I AM,

The Secret to Contentment

I bring greetings and love to each one of you this day. I am the energy that Laughing Heart calls Grandmother.

Today, I have a secret to share with you. It is Simplicity. Simplicity is the key to contentment. The less you are able to get along with, the easier your life will be. The more material things you possess, the more complicated your life becomes. There is more for you to worry about losing. If you need only what is necessary to live on, you will always have enough. If you need material things, you are constantly striving to get them. You will never be in a place of security and rest because of the more you get, the more you want . . . the more you think you need.

I am not telling you that material possessions are bad or that Spirit doesn't want you to have them. Indeed, Spirit desires for you to have anything you wish to have. But your old saying; "be careful what you wish for" certainly applies here. Focus, instead, on the spiritual aspects of your life and the other things will follow.

In the days to come, your economy is going to continue to change and shift. The energy of your money is going to change form. Barter and trade will be the more common way of doing business. The old ways will return and people will remember how it used to be. Technology has brought many wonderful inventions to your planet and was meant to be a blessing. But in excess, it has caused you to lose many of the gifts of humanity. A return to simplicity will serve you well in the days to come.

With Love, I AM simply,

Grandmother

Symptoms of the Ascension

Aho, and greetings to you all. My heart is filled with love as I come once again to speak to you.

I see that many of you are experiencing what has been called by some, symptoms of the ascension. This has been a concern to some of you as your moods are shifting rapidly from one extreme to another and your energy level has been lower than usual, sometimes interspersed with great bursts of frenetic energy that is hard to contain. Be assured that this is a transitory occurrence and nothing to fret over. Among other things you may be experiencing physical symptoms that are similar to what you call the flu. There may be a great deal of stuff from your past that is being dredged up. You ask yourself "Why is this here again"? There is a cleansing, or clearing, that is taking place now. Anything that holds the slightest bit of a charge from your past is being moved up and out of your subconscious, in order for you to continue your alteration into a place of higher vibrational frequency. This clearing out process can make your physical vehicle tired and in need of much solitude and quietness. Indeed, you may find yourself unable to be in the energy field of others as this deep modification is taking place inside of you. Honor these emotions and needs as they come. Give your self the space to accommodate the inner changes. Also, be aware that this is happening to everyone, so give others the space that they need also. Friends may draw away from one another for a period of time and your relationships will perhaps be a bit strained. Respect what is occurring in your own life and the lives of those around you. Try not to take things personally and do not be offended if you feel slighted. All will come into balance. As I have told you before, balance is not optional, it is necessary. Your energy will level out and your friends will be drawn into your life again, if it is meant to be so. This point in your quickening is solitary, meaning that only you can do your own work, but know that **you are never alone.**

In Love, I AM,

Grandmother

Your Earth Walk

Greetings dear ones and much love to each of you I bring. I am the energy that Laughing Heart calls Grandmother.

I would like to shed a bit of light on a subject that some of you have difficulty with. You have all heard the teaching, I am sure, that you can manifest whatever you wish, be totally enlightened and be in tune with God at all times, or teachings similar to these. Now, on the very highest spiritual frequency this is Truth. However, there seems to be some confusion as to how this happens in your present reality of the Earth Walk you have chosen. Remember that you chose this walk for the purpose of learning how to love and for the purpose of experiencing and becoming Joy. In order to accomplish these things there needs to be a catalyst for the lessons to occur.

There is no need to struggle or condemn yourself when you seem to fall short of the goals that these teachings say are "a done deal." (Is this the correct phrase?) All learning is a process and until you actually reach the next plane of existence, you are subject to the circumstances and conditions that are here on your planet. Were you to reach that level of existence, you would no longer require a physical body and would transition to the spirit world. So the struggles and challenges you face are not due to a lack of faith, or because you are not enlightened or spiritual enough. They are designed to bring you ever closer to that state of being, which is what you are as a spiritual being, but have not yet completed as a physical being.

So, children, be at peace, be gentle with yourselves and relax into being who and what you are here on Earth. And trust that you are *becoming* here who you already are in the spirit realm.

With Love, I AM,

Grandmother

Divine Order

Greetings to each of you, I come to speak with joy in my heart and with appreciation for each individual soul that is hungry and seeking for truth today. I am the energy that Laughing Heart calls Grandmother.

You are living in exciting times, as well you know. The world is changing rapidly and in significant ways. It can feel overwhelming at times and you wonder if there is an anchor to which you can hold. Something that you can rely on to keep you grounded in the Truth; something solid to stand upon while all else appears to be unstable and shaky. Creator's love, as demonstrated in the model of Divine Order, is the anchor that you can hold onto.

Knowing that Divine Order does not falter and does not change is the cornerstone on which you can safely and securely build your life. In the midst of seeming chaos and in the tremendous economic shifts that are daily occurring, rest in the fact that Divine Order is the highest vibration of Truth. The crumbling structures of your economy, yes, even the shifting of your entire society, is not something for you to fear. Divine Order says to you that Creator has a Plan and you are a part of it. Divine Order says that even though times can be difficult in this realm, in the spirit realm all is going according to the arrangement. Divine Order says that no matter what outward circumstances show, nothing happens to you that does not have a purpose and a reason. There is NOTHING that Creator cannot take, and use for the highest good of your soul. Even events that seem tragic to those looking on can be transformed and used to bring a deeper experience of Creator's love and compassion.

I invite you at all times and in every situation, to remind yourself that Divine Order is one of the many ways that Creator expresses His/Her love for you. I realize that these words are often tossed around lightly and sometimes used by others to deny the intensity of your personal situations. Let them take on new meaning for you today. The words "everything is in Divine Order" are not just a new age catch phrase. These words convey Spiritual Reality. Hold them in your heart and draw comfort and strength from them.

With Love,

I AM,

Grandmother

Being a Woman

Greetings to you all. I am the energy that Laughing Heart calls Grandmother, and I come in love.

This is indeed a wonderful time to be a woman. Not since the ancient days of goddess worship have women been in such a position of empowerment. Never before have you been able to share your innate (and acquired) gifts so freely and in such a public arena without fear of retribution. Had you done so in the past, you would have faced, at best, public humiliation and punishment and at worst you would have been hanged as a witch. Today, women everywhere are finding their personal power and learning to stand in their own truth. (Some of you **were** hanged as witches, but that is a message for another day.) (Smile)

The feminine energy is flooding your planet as never before. The old patriarchal paradigm is crumbling and dissolving, as it needs to. In its place will be born a perfect blending of the two energies and from this center of balance the new paradigm of love and light will spring forth. For a brief period, the feminine energy will predominate, as the masculine energy has done for so long. But at the right time, the center will be found and balance will occur. Just as a pendulum swings back and forth from one side to the other, going from one extreme to another, so must the energies swing until balance is reached.

This is also an empowering time for men. As the patriarchy falls away, men are awakening to the knowing that there has been (and still is in some cases) an energetic imbalance. Many of them do not know what to do in place of this old pattern of behavior, even though they recognize that it does not serve the highest good. They have no idea what "getting in touch with their feminine side" means and it actually sounds frightening to many of them. It sounds emasculating, as though they have to stop being a man in order to do this. Understanding this fear may help you deal with the men in your life in a more compassionate manner. As women, you can illuminate their paths by example much better than you can by trying to "teach" them, or by trying to persuade them to change. You know this statement to be truth (Smile). Let your own life be balanced with a blend of both energies, and they will see that both energies are present in all beings and will not be so afraid of it. As you hold this vibrational balance in your personal lives, you are helping to anchor the energies and provide a space for the center to be found on a global scale. **Yes, this is how important each one of you are individually.**

Let Me elaborate on the interactions you have with the men in your life. Do not let their seeming indifference to matters of the spirit disturb you. Things are never as they seem on the surface, remember. Know that things are moving along in Divine Order. The feminine energy that is flooding your planet is causing much discomfort to some of the males that you are dealing with. They are unaware at this point of what is causing the disruption in their energy fields. They may react to situations in ways that seem less than spiritual to you. Do not be alarmed or discouraged. The balance will shift and the energy will level out. Use these interactions as points of learning and opportunities for growth.

Don't misunderstand. I am telling none of my daughters to stay in an abusive relationship. But do have patience with the significant males that are in your life. In the meantime, they do present many opportunities for expansion, do they not? (Smile)

Walk in Balance,

Grandmother

Needs versus Desires

Greetings and love to each of you. I am, as you know, the energy that Laughing Heart calls Grandmother

These are perilous times that you are facing. Events are culminating in the process that has been occurring for a long time and is known to many as the Ascension. It has been called various names by different cultures, but all are speaking of the same event, or process of events, I should say. Yes, these times are perilous indeed, but let me be quick to say that there is no reason to fear. Creator has promised to provide for all of your needs. Many of you are discovering that your needs are much different than you previously thought; is this not true? You are finding that you can survive and indeed thrive, on much less than you thought?

This is a very good lesson to learn, my children. Now, there is a mindset that says you can also have all of your **desires** fulfilled simply by thinking it to be so. Has this been true in your experience, or do you still have unmet desires? If so, consider this . . . the desires that you have for joy, love, peace, truth and light are always met. It does not take a great deal of effort on your part for this to be so. Your desires for material possessions may not be met so quickly, no matter how hard you try to attract them by positive thinking. Desires are different from needs and the things that you desire may not always be what are for your highest good and your souls' best interest. It is okay to have material things as long as you own them and they do not own you. Hold on to your material possessions lightly and with a loose hand. Now is a good time to cut back and see what you can do without. Do not be fearful, but do be wise. Understand that the things which are real can never be lost or taken from you. When you think positively with all your strength and your desires seem to go unfulfilled, instead of beating yourself up for failing at manifesting, consider that your desires are perhaps not as essential as your needs at this point. Trust that your needs will all be supplied and get a higher perspective on what your desires are. Desire the attributes of spirit that will aid in the evolution of your soul and that will assist your planet in her course of healing.

With Great Love,

Grandmother

Concerning Matter

Greetings to you one and all. I come today with much love and much joy, to speak of a subject of great interest and importance in your life. I am, as you are aware, the energy that Laughing Heart knows as Grandmother. If this is a good visual for you, feel free to address me in like manner. If not, visualize me in whatever form is comforting for you. Are we ready? Yes? Good, then let us begin.

The word "matter" in your language can be used in several ways. It can be used as a noun, meaning "something that has form and substance." If it is matter, then you can see, touch and feel it; be affected by it, if you will. It can also be used as a verb, "to matter", meaning to take on form and substance. When something exists in the void (where all things are born), or on another realm of spirit and is not yet manifested here in the physical, then it has not yet mattered. It has not yet taken on form and substance, so it is not yet matter. Do you understand this? Whether or not something matters is up to you. You are the one that makes a thing, or a situation, in your life matter. You bring it into form and give it substance, with the power of your imagination and your intention. Do not let the word imagination cause you to stumble. It simply means to create an image of something your mind, usually an image of something you have not seen before. So, dear ones, you form an image in your mind (imagine it) of whatever it is that you want. Then, with the power of your intention, bring it into form and make it matter! On the other side of the coin, when faced with a challenging circumstance, ask yourself the question "Does this really matter?" The answer is completely up to you. Does it? Does it really matter to you? If you don't want it to, it doesn't have to.

(Just as an aside. Another good question to ask your self if something undesired has already "mattered" is this: How much will this matter ten years from now in light of eternity?) But that is a teaching for another day. (Smile)

Until the next time.

I AM,

Grandmother

Experiencing Both Sides of the Coin

Greetings, children. I come to you in peace. I feel joy at meeting with you all once again and have love in my heart. I think that perhaps I will raise a few eyebrows with this message today, but that is okay, is it not? Maybe some eyebrows need to be raised, yes? (Smile) I have watched many of you struggle with the teachings today that tell you everything must always be perfect and that your path must be flower-strewn and full of happiness at every turn. If it is not, then this is entirely your fault due to your negative thinking, or your failure to visualize the proper outcome, or whatever the case may be. They would tell you that you are living at a much lower level than those who have such a life. (Those who tell you they live in this state of constant happiness and bliss are being dishonest with you and with themselves). Furthermore, for a "small fee" someone is willing to give you the perfect formula, share with you the right ceremony or prayer, or teach you the positive affirmation that guarantees your prolonged and permanent state of happiness. This state of being exists not on your Earth plane, my children.

Happiness is contingent upon your outward circumstances and as you know, circumstances can be quite challenging here in this realm of reality. **Joy however, can be experienced at all times. In spite of and not because of, outward circumstances.** As I have often told you, balance is a spiritual principle that is absolutely necessary. It exists in nature and in all things. It exists in the spirit realm. "As above so below", yes? Then consider that without sadness, grief, or sorrow, you would have nothing to measure your happiness by. If you knew not what lack is, could you be as abundantly grateful for all that you do have?

Hear me now. You have chosen to take on a denser vibration in order to become flesh for the express purpose of experiencing emotions and learning lessons to hasten and heighten your soul's evolution. Do you not think that *all* emotion must be experienced in order for your mission to be successful? Not just the pleasant ones? When you have received all knowledge and have reached the fullest potential for this lifetime you will have no further need of this body. Until then, there needs to be an experience of the Balance that exists in all things and on all levels of creation. I am not speaking of duality here; for indeed all things are part of the same Oneness, therefore there can be no true duality. There is however, how do you say, two sides to the coin? Both sides must be experienced for you to effectively re-member yourself, that is put yourself back together, which is what remembering is.

When facing a hurdle in your Earth walk, recall the word **Balance** to your mind. Know that any challenge can be met with grace and strength, with the knowledge that Creator has much love for you. Know that the ebb and flow of the human experience, both sides of the coin of human life are essential for your growth. Above all, trust in the absolute goodness of Creator.

With love,

Grandmother

Life Exists Eternally

There is a vibration of fear and panic that has been released into the energy field of the Earth recently. It is going out primarily through the airwaves, but people are accepting it into their personal energy fields and feeding it with their belief. In this way it is being passed more rapidly from one place to another. I urge you to stand firm in the face of this fear and KNOW that **all is well**. Creator has everything under control. It is true that challenging times lie ahead for Earth and her people. But this is a natural part of the purification that is taking place. As one cycle ends and another begins, there will be an intensifying energy of purging. This is nothing to fear and it is all part of the greater Plan. Those souls who have chosen to leave the planet during this time will do so and will continue to assist in the process from another dimension. The souls that have chosen to stay and see the process through to the end, will do so, and will continue to assist in the process from this plane. The biggest fear that you feel comes from your misunderstanding of death. When you hear reports of people dying, this produces fear. Fear for yourselves and for your loved ones. But when you realize that death does not exist, then you know there is nothing to fear. Nothing ever dies, it only changes form. All life is eternal and will continue to exist in one form or another. Some souls have chosen to transition by way of natural disaster or disease but this is not a "tragedy." It is simply the way of departure that they have chosen on a soul level. If a soul has made a contract to leave the Earth plane at a particular time, then when that time is ripe the soul will depart this plane. It will do so in whatever manner has been chosen or even in whatever manner is available. If the time for a soul to leave has not yet arrived, then that soul will continue to live in this Earth plane until that time comes.

If I may put it more succinctly; when it is your time to die . . . remember this is just a change of form, you will do so. If it is not your time to change form, then you will not, no matter what the circumstances are around you. As the days and months ahead become more uncertain, rest in the knowing that your path is already mapped out and is being orchestrated by divine forces. You are not the victim of random circumstances, except to a small degree. Creator sees the big picture. You have seen it too . . . or you would not have chosen to be here in such difficult times. The world is not coming to an end. It is simply finishing one cycle and beginning another. **All is well**, you are loved.

In peace,

I AM,

Grandmother

Mother Earth ~ A Living Being

Greetings to you, and much love from my heart. I am the energy that Laughing Heart calls Grandmother. I am just one ray of the Great Light that comprises the Oneness of All That Is. I have chosen to express myself in this manner for the purpose of bringing guidance, strength, wisdom, knowledge and love to any and all, who wish to receive these things. The message today is of vital importance, so I ask you to open your hearts to hear it.

The ancient ones had a deep and strong connection to the Earth. They knew and understood that She is a living, sentient being with an intelligent awareness. They were taught to love and respect Her from an early age. Sadly this connection has been lost for many people. Unfortunately, the Church has been one of the biggest contributors to this way of thinking. The Earth is looked upon as something to be dominated, subdued, used, controlled and divided into parcels to be fought over. However, your ancestors understood that the Earth does not belong to man, but rather man belongs to the Earth. Mother Earth could exist without humans and could sustain herself in perfect balance. But humans could not exist without Her. Great Spirit created the Earth with a spirit, a consciousness and a life force just as every being was created. Mankind was given the privilege and the divine responsibility to care for Her, to live in harmony with Her and all Her relations. The waters are Her blood, the grasses and herbs are Her hair, the rocks and mountains are Her breasts and Her bones. **She is alive!**

It is time to remember the way it used to be. It's time to return to the old path before it is too late. Mother Earth has been patient and has given Her gifts freely and generously, but She is tired and in need of healing. She has been depleted and has been used carelessly without thought for the generations of children yet to be born.

The first thing that must change is your attitude toward the Earth. Cultivate a sense of gratitude for all that She provides for you. And express thanks to Her. **She hears and will respond.** As your attitude changes, so will your actions follow suit. Walk gently upon the Earth. Never take more than you need. Leave Her an offering out of respect whenever you gather or harvest. Listen to the pulse of Her heartbeat, feel Her rhythms and learn how to be in sync with Her cycles. Tune into the songs of the trees, the humming of the plants and the drumming of the rocks. They are all messengers that carry a piece of Great Sprit and a vibration of life within themselves.

When you realize (make real) this truth, you will never again be able to view Mother Earth as a lifeless object existing just for the purpose of being used by humankind. You will see that She has graciously chosen to give of Her self to support the life forms that exist upon Her back. She is a Being who allows you to receive your sustenance from Her body. Today is Earth Day . . . Honor Her.

Love,

Grandmother

Mother's Day Message

To each of you who are mothers, I am wishing blessings of peace and joy upon you today. Your responsibility is a very important one and your privilege is great. To those of you who are not mothers in the physical sense, you are still life bearers and givers of birth. As women, you are blessed beyond measure.

Honor your own mothers today whether they are still in this realm or have already changed form. Honor them whether they provided you with all that you needed or not. For to honor your mother, is to honor yourself as women. Men; honor the mother that you chose to be the physical vehicle that brought you into this plane. Recognize that without her, you could not have taken on physical form.

For those of you who have wounds that are still in need of healing, I invite you, just for today, to lay them aside and be thankful for all that your mother **did** do. Explore the idea that perhaps she did the best she could with what knowledge and opportunity she had at the time you were growing up under her care. Offer her the acceptance and forgiveness you would wish to receive from your own children.

Honor your Earth Mother today and appreciate her nurturing care and provision for you. Honor yourselves as mothers and life-givers. Know that Creator recognizes what a tremendous amount of time, love, and patience is required to be a mother.

And finally, understand that the love you feel for your children is but a speck compared to the great love that Creator has for each of you.

Aho, I AM,

Grandmother

Holiday Message

Greetings and love to you all. I am, as you know, the energy that Laughing Heart calls Grandmother.

As your holidays draw near, I have noticed that your stress levels have risen. Indeed, the season that you, as humans, have chosen to be one of the happiest seems, instead, to be the most stress inducing. I find this most interesting and I desire for you to experience your holy days in a different manner.

Remember firstly, that every day is a holy day. Each day that you walk upon Earth Mother is sacred and is intended to bring you joy. Each day is as holy as the next one and this season is no more special than any other, truthfully. However, I understand that in your realm of existence, this time is set apart for special celebration. I invite you to experience it in a different way now that you have become more aware and enlightened. Most of your stress comes from the focus that is put upon material possessions. Even the desire to give to others can produce stress if you to not have the means to do this. Try instead to find ways of giving that do not require the spending of your money. Let your spirit tell you what you can provide for someone else through a kind word, an understanding heart or a listening, non-judgmental ear. Material possessions are not "bad", they are simply temporary. There are other gifts that will last forever. The gifts of love, acceptance, forgiveness, compassion, friendship and tolerance are a few examples of this kind of gift.

Whatever tradition you choose to honor in this season and however you choose to honor Spirit in that tradition is proper and appropriate if it brings you joy. Remember that joy is what your "holy days" are all about! The monetary value of a gift is not what gives it meaning, nor is it a measurement of your love for the person you are gifting. Take this truth inside of you and make it your own. It has the power to liberate you.

Wishing you stress-free and joyful Holy Days,

I AM,

Grandmother

Layers of Reality

Nothing is ever as it appears to be on the surface. There are many layers of reality and generally you see only the top layer. That is the one that is expressed physically and is most perceptible to your human eyes. But there are many more layers beneath this one, or perhaps it is more accurate to say they are above this reality, not beneath it. Each layer is vibrating at a different speed, or level. The higher or faster frequencies are more difficult for you to see. You can raise your own vibrational frequency to match that of the higher dimension, or the beings there can choose to lower their own in order to be seen. But it is easier for you to raise yours than it is for them to lower theirs. This physical energy (here on Earth) is dense enough that it has congealed into "matter" and become visible to human eyes. This is how your physical body was born. Your spirit came from the highest level of reality, traveled through many layers, each one becoming more dense and heavy and finally took on the density of human form. Your spirit did this willingly in order to have the experiences that you have each had. Now, while you are here in this "mattered" form, you exist with the qualities that exist here. You have physical "limitations" or boundaries that are set in place. These serve a purpose, but they are only an illusion. If you can remember at all times that this reality is an illusion, a fantasy, if you will, it will not be as difficult to deal with some of the situations that arise. You are taking part in a cosmic drama and are playing the role that your soul assigned to itself. Everyone in your life, indeed, everyone period is doing the same. Look beyond the illusion and find the higher truth behind it. You have the ability to do this, you all do. The limitations and boundaries are only things that you put into place to challenge yourself. Challenge yourself to break free from the illusion and to see behind the scenes of the drama that is occurring here on Earth. You created the illusion . . . You can dissolve it.

With great love,
I AM,

Grandmother

Vortexes in the Earth

Your planet has many energetic centers that may be referred to as vortexes. The word vortex pertains more to the cone shape of these energy centers than anything else. These centers are akin to the chakras in the human body. They are places of energy that is swirling in a downward motion and creating a "cone" of power and energetic momentum that helps to keep the Earth on her orbital pattern. Just as the human body has many centers that might be called "pressure points," as in acupuncture or acupressure, so also does your Earth Mother. Some of these places that people call vortexes are actually places where thousands of years of ceremony have taken place and the energy has collected into such a magnitude of power that people can actually feel it. Other centers are centers of energy that have been there in the Earth since her inception. These vortexes were placed there for a specific purpose. They will be opened, or activated, as the need arises and as the time is right. Yes, you as human beings can help to open these vortexes with your prayers and with your intentions. But they will be opened with or without your help, for that is the plan and that is their purpose. They are here to assist in the great shift that is so rapidly approaching. But when you do assist in their opening it will benefit you greatly and will help to hasten the process.

In this way it will benefit you . . . As they open up, more and more energy will be brought into your atmosphere from the etheric plane and from other dimensions. These energies will be filled with light, information and with much healing power. Some of these vortex centers will be "portals" for other beings to contact your race through. Indeed, these portals have been open and active for many years, but most of the population has not been ready to accept the presence of "others." Sadly, many of the human race would be quick to kill and destroy any life form that they are not familiar with. This is mainly due to fear.

Humankind has such an enormous collective ego that many actually believe that they are the only form of life in the whole enormous, constantly expanding universe. How ridiculous! Of the many different forms of life as there are on your planet alone, these are a mere speck of the life that exists outside of your experience. The love of God is so great that it can extend to as many beings as you could ever possibly imagine and even more. You need to expand your mind and your concept of whom and what God is . . . then believe beyond even that limitation.

In light & love,

Grandmother

The Vibration of Love

Greetings, Dear Ones, I speak peace to you. I am the energy that Laughing Heart calls Grandmother. It is with great joy that I come again. I have missed being in communication with you. Laughing Heart and I have been alone for a time and she is weakened physically, but I have strengthened her spiritually in a good way. Please be patient with my hollow bone as she attempts to integrate the changes that have occurred inside of her.

Children, I tell you that time, as you know it, has been greatly accelerated since the new energies of solstice have come through. It is time for you to raise your vibration of love to a new level. It is necessary. You **must** do this in order to bring the changes to completion for the Earth and Her peoples. Love is what is needed in order for the ascension of your planet to fully take place. Love for yourselves, love for each other and love for all your relations. Love must rise in your hearts and your spirits must resonate with the unconditional love of Creator for all beings. When you begin to see each other as extensions of yourself and know in your deepest being that you are all One, then the climate for the Shift will be right and the evolution will be complete. As you pursue your passions and strive to find the work that you have come to do to assist in the coming change, know that LOVE is what you are all here to accomplish and to experience. Only in love can the work be done.

Fighting against what is occurring, as though it is some imagined "enemy" is futile. Whatever you fight against only becomes stronger as you feed energy into it by focusing on it. Do not fear as you see the old world pass away and the old paradigms become extinct. Everything must crumble in order to make way for the new systems to become functional. Love is the foundation upon which the new constructs will be based and built. As you vibrate with the frequency of Love, for yourself, for others and for all beings, you will automatically be raised up to meet the new frequency that is just above you, only a microscopic measure past your physical sight. As you raise yourself in frequency and the new paradigm lowers itself to fall upon you, you will meet there in the space of unconditional love and set firmly in place a new way of existing.

You must let go of all psychic ties to people and circumstances that have hurt you or caused you harm in any way. Release them into the healing light of unconditional love, for they are here to play their ordained roles in the growth of your soul. Forgive your own self for any "failures" that you are holding onto, for you also have played the part of "lesson bringer" to many in your life. You are all here to help one another and to set up the perfect conditions needed for the great Awakening to occur. This has been accomplished in many ways, all of which were meant to be played out just as they were, for there are no mistakes in your life.

Rest in this Truth,

Grandmother

What is Harmony?

Greetings and love to you, I bring. I am the energy that Laughing Heart calls Grandmother. I wish to share with you some thoughts on Harmony. Harmony is not, as you may think, two notes that sound exactly the same. Harmony occurs when two different notes are played or sung together, blending to make a pleasing sound. There might be a low note and a high note, a sharp note and a flat note, a half note and a whole note and so forth. These two notes are vibrating at a different frequency in order to make their individual sounds, but when played together they blend into a "harmony." Harmony exists when two or more notes that are different are put together and used to form a sound that is fuller and richer than the one note would have been alone. So it is in relationships. When two or more people are joined together, even though they may be on different frequencies, they can sing a beautiful harmonious song. The song will be fuller and richer than one they might have sung alone. There is a time to sing alone and a time to join the chorus! Now is the time to join the chorus and make a harmonious whole that can begin to heal your planet. I am speaking of spiritual matters here. It is time to put aside your differences, concentrate on common beliefs and compose a song of harmony to sing your planet back into alignment with the universe. Forgiveness also plays a large part of the process of bringing about Harmony. Holding a grudge, or holding onto resentment and anger is a discordant note in the song that now needs to be sung for the healing of your planet. Forgive yourself and others. Release the past into the Light and open your hearts to join voices with all of mankind to sing balance into being.

Your mass consciousness is one of lack, scarcity, pain, sorrow, greed, war and poverty. It is time to sing a song of wholeness, completeness, healing, joy, tranquility and love. It is time to be a channel for the Light that is coming into your universal consciousness. Each time you have a loving thought toward someone else, or send up a prayer for healing, or refuse to judge, you are helping the Light to burn brighter. You are all assisting the planet to be reborn into a new state of being. She is returning to her original state of well being. I tell you that Mother Earth was created into a state of total health and wholeness; it is the actions of humans that have caused Her to be in the state She is in today. I am not judging or scolding now. I am simply telling you how things are so that you can assist with bringing them back to where they were meant to be. In the beginning, Mother Earth had all that you needed to survive. She produced all the plants, herbs for healing and food that were necessary for your survival. As you became denser and denser in your form, vibrated at a slower rate and became stuck in "matter," you gradually lost the ability to see things as they really are. You began to think in terms of lack and greed and such. This has continued unto this present age and is going to change in a very short amount of time as you know it. As Mother Earth has been used and misused for so many years, She is depleted of Her original resources. The fear of not having enough has caused many to gather more than they need.

As more and more people and nations did this, the Earth began to run out of provisions. Now you are indeed in a state of lack. This is what the greed and fear have caused to happen. I tell you that when you begin to live from a place of abundance and plenty, the situation will change. As more and more people change their vibration to one of harmony and move away from the notion of "mine" and "yours", and indeed come from a place of "ours", **Mother Earth can and will, replenish Her self.**

Much Love to all,

I AM,

Grandmother

A Final Word

Aho, children. I come as the bearer of love and peace. I would like to bring one last message for this book. A kind of "summary" I think you would say?

As always, I am honored to be here to bring a message to you.

Each one of you is changing at an extremely rapid pace. Some of the changes have felt physically and emotionally overwhelming, yes? Be assured that you are not alone in this process. You are being called to a higher consciousness, as well as being fashioned into containers that can hold more Light than you have ever held before. The Light that is breaking on your planet is of such magnitude that you would be unable to hold it if your bodies were not being re-aligned for this purpose. I have brought this message, or similar ones, many times before. But people need to hear it again and again in order to make it their Truth.

The message is this . . . Love is the most powerful force that exists. Love is what will carry you safely through the Shift and bring you into the new reality. Love is absolutely necessary. Leaving love out of the equation is not an option. All of the crises that you face, all of the Earth changes that are, and will continue to occur, the failing economy, the escalation of "evil," the appearance of tragedy and disaster, all of these things can and will be weathered if you carry the vibration of Love in your hearts.

As mankind makes this tremendous leap in its collective spiritual evolution, all of these events must take place. As I have said before, each of you individually, all of you collectively and your whole planet, is going through a deep purging and cleansing process. Anything which still resides in your subconscious that might impede your progress must be brought up and exposed to the Light. You are being asked to willingly surrender any and all old habits, beliefs and behaviors that will not serve you in the new Consciousness that is dawning. You must be aware of these issues before you can release them, so circumstances are being called into play by your soul to create spaces for this to happen. Some of the occurrences in your lives recently have been extremely trying for many of you. Let me clarify that "bad things" haven't been caused or created by your soul, but any and all means will be used to aid in the purging of your subconscious.

Your physical bodies are actually changing. Your food preferences and your sleeping patterns are being altered. Your relationships are changing. People that you thought would be in your life forever have moved away and you have moved on. New friends and different people are coming into your lives and often there is an immediate recognition between you. These are souls that you have contracted with for a specific purpose at this precise time.

Hold your possessions and yes, your relationships loosely. For some of them will come and go rapidly during this in-between period. Time is escalating and issues will be resolved, lessons will be given and learned. Healings will happen at a quickened pace. This is as it should be, so do not be alarmed.

Remember that the Earth is a living Being, with a consciousness and a sense of awareness. Walk upon Her gently and reverently. Treat Her respectfully. Take time to connect with Her and feel Her energy that has the ability to replenish your own energy. Remember the ways of the Ancient Ones and follow them as closely as you are able. Recognize the sacredness of all creatures and honor them as your co-inhabitants upon the blessed Earth Mother.

Tend to the young ones. Teach them with words and by your actions. The children being born today are special indeed. They are here to assist in the Ascension process in a very unique way. Encourage them to develop their gifts and hone their innate abilities. Realize that their imaginary friends and their fantasies are, more likely than not, real beings and real experiences. The veil between the worlds is very thin today and children can walk through it much easier than most adults.

Walk in balance. Do not be so "spiritual" that you are helpless or useless in the physical world. Do not be so "worldly" that you cannot accept and experience the beauty of the spiritual realm. Do not take an extreme position on any issue, for things are shifting so quickly that what is your truth today may not be your truth tomorrow. Be open. Be flexible, but do not believe everything you hear. Weigh any messages (mine included), by the eternal Truth of Creator's love for you. Know that there are many different paths and refrain from judging any one of them as being better than another. In like manner, there are many modalities of healing, many traditions of ceremony and many forms of prayer. Do whatever feels right to you and always do it with right intention. Keep your intentions pure and do not come from a place of ego. Know how wonderful and beautiful you truly are, but understand that each of you is equally wonderful and beautiful.

Do not be fearful of all the changes that are happening around and within you. Know that Divine Order is a Spiritual Truth. The words, "Everything is as it should be" are not just empty words. They convey a solid, divine Truth that you can put your complete trust and faith in. When storms are raging around you, hold fast to the anchor of this Truth. Let it keep you firmly planted in Spiritual Reality and not stuck in the Great Illusion that is the third dimension.

Know that you are loved. Know that you have great worth and value in the eyes of Creator. You each have an integral part to play in the unfolding of this new age of peace. Holding the frequency of Love in your heart is essential in bringing this age of peace into being. Holding the love vibration does not mean that you will like everyone and everything in your path. It does not mean that you will want to have everyone you meet and everything you experience stay in your life. It means that you make the choice not to pass judgment, not to criticize (no, not even "constructively" criticize), others for their actions, decisions, or beliefs. It means that you will value each other for what you are inside, not how much you have, or how you look, or who you know or what you do for a living. It means that you will put aside dividing boundaries of race, creed and the color of your skin. It means that you must begin to see the Earth as a whole, and not separated into sections of "ours" and "theirs". It means embracing all of humankind as one family. That is what you truly are, for Creator is the Divine Parent of all beings.

I have left you with much to think about, yes? Ah, good, than my purpose was served. As always, take what resonates with you and disregard the rest. I only ask that perhaps you would consider coming back at another time. Something that didn't apply to you today may possibly do so tomorrow. Remember, nothing is permanent except Change. (Smile)

With tender love, and great excitement over the future,

I AM,

Grandmother

Contact Laughing Heart at:

eaglehors1@gmail.com

Laughing Heart is an ordained minister in The Brigade of Light, and offers all ministerial services.

As a Medicine Woman in the tradition of Rainbow Medicine, she offers sacred ceremonies in the Native American tradition as well as Soul Retrievals.

As Grandmother's hollow bone, she offers individual and/or group sessions, readings and counseling. Phone consultations are also available, as are private soul messages via e-mail.

Contact Laughing Heart at:

eaglehors1@gmail.com

Laughing Heart is an ordained minister in The Brigade of Light, and offers all ministerial services.

As a Medicine Woman in the tradition of Rainbow Medicine, she offers sacred ceremonies in the Native American tradition as well as Soul Retrievals.

As Grandmother's hollow bone, she offers individual and/or group sessions, readings and counseling. Phone consultations are also available, as are private soul messages via e-mail.

Donna
832-781-
9040

LaVergne, TN USA
07 March 2011
219118LV00001B/2/P